r and precious father an act of goodness
od shows the man, as r vs
ndino wisdom begins in wonder socrates the
ple say you cannot do it's good to be queen each
ive to be foremost in good deeds benjamin
eek proverb our first teacher is our own heart
ook up is joy confucius the future belongs to
eams eleanor roosevelt where there is love there
ou are seeking is in yourself little minds achieve
ook keep company with those who make
st possession benjamin franklin we shall light a
put out anonymous love is the river of life in
dream to create the future victor hugo a life
proverb grow old along with me the best is
were as long as twenty days are now

W9-BOM-990

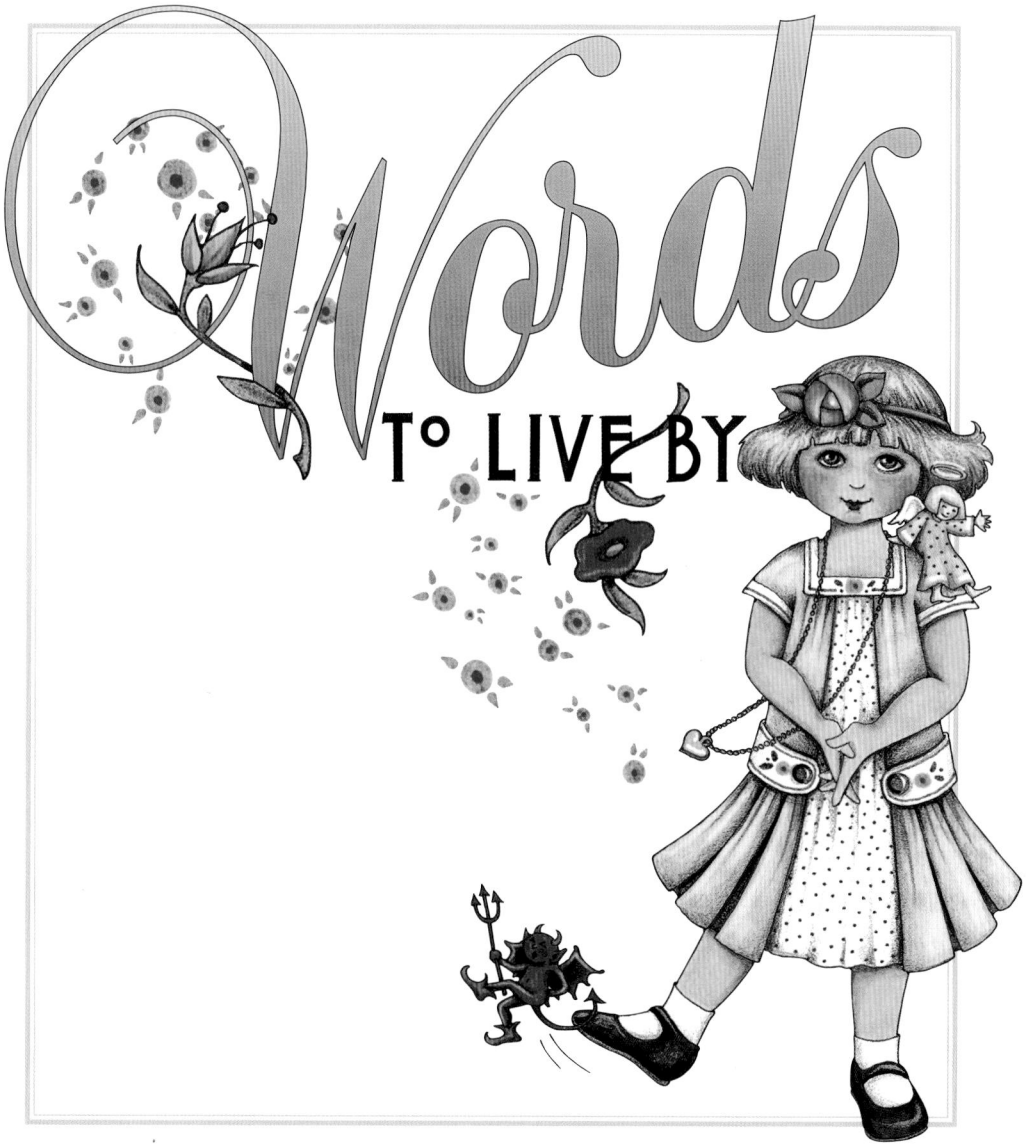
Words
TO LIVE BY

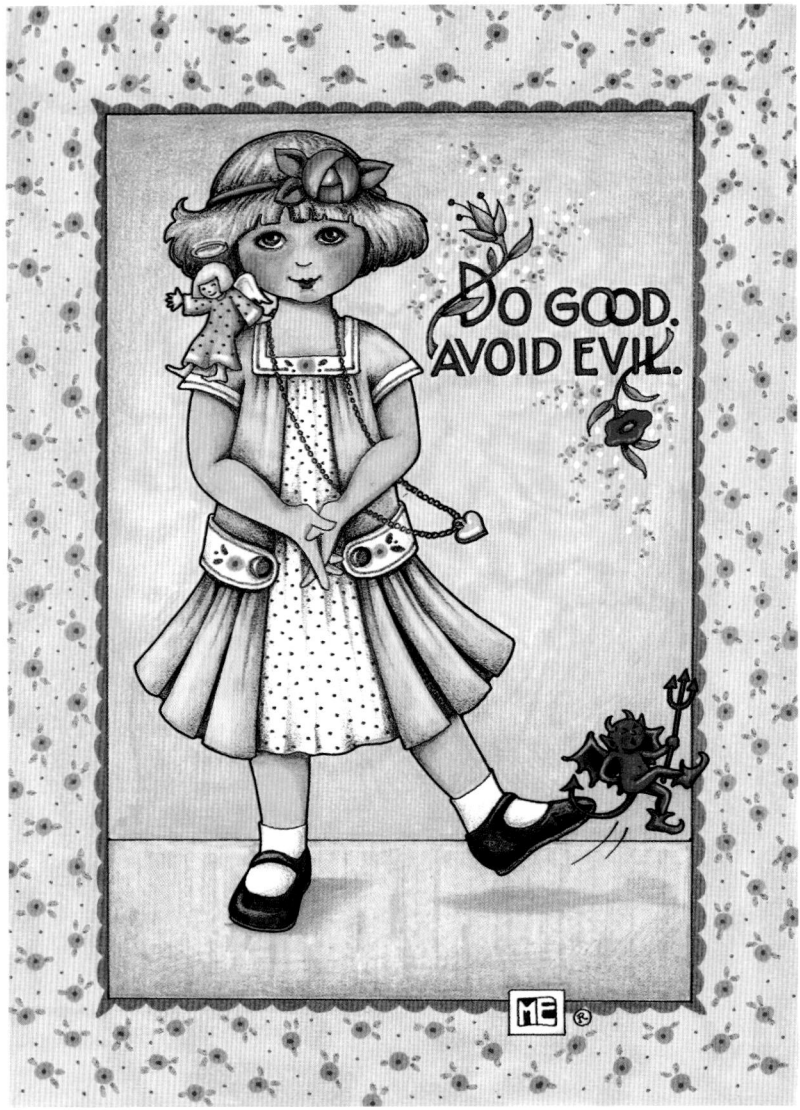
DO GOOD.
AVOID EVIL.
ME ®

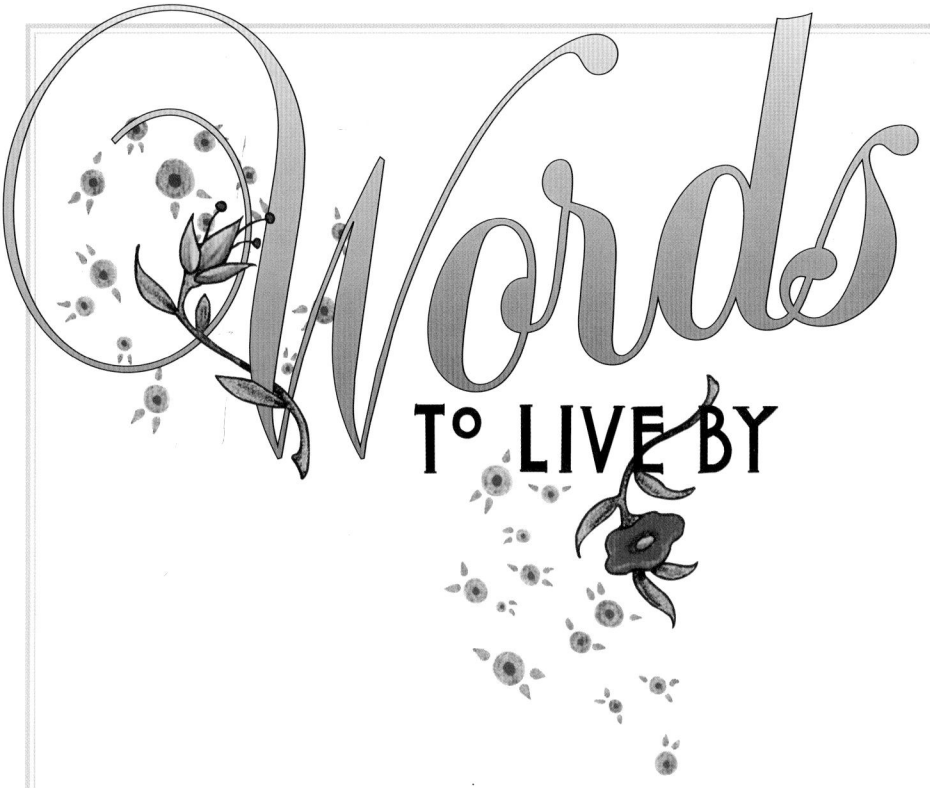

illustrated by Mary Engelbreit

Andrews McMeel Publishing

Kansas City

Words to Live By copyright © 1999 by Mary Engelbreit Ink. All rights reserved. Printed in Italy. No part of this book may be used or reproduced in any manner whatsoever without written permission except in the case of reprints in the context of reviews. For information write Andrews McMeel Publishing, an Andrews McMeel Universal company, 4520 Main Street, Kansas City, Missouri 64111.

www.andrewsmcmeel.com
www.maryengelbreit.com

is a registered trademark of Mary Engelbreit Enterprises, Inc.

Words to live by / illustrated by Mary Engelbreit.
p. cm.
ISBN 0-7407-0028-6
1. Conduct of life Quotations, maxims, etc. I. Engelbreit, Mary.
PN6084.C556W67 1999
082--dc21 99-37116
CIP

Edited by Jean Lowe
Design by Stephanie R. Farley

ATTENTION: SCHOOLS AND BUSINESSES
Andrews McMeel books are available at quantity discounts with bulk purchase for educational, business, or sales promotional use. For information, please write to: Special Sales Department, Andrews McMeel Publishing, 4520 Main Street, Kansas City, Missouri 64111.

Contents

Introduction...7

Words to Live By...

...from great writers • 9

...from great spiritual guides • 29

...from great thinkers • 43

...from word of mouth • 61

...from folk wisdom • 79

A few Words...

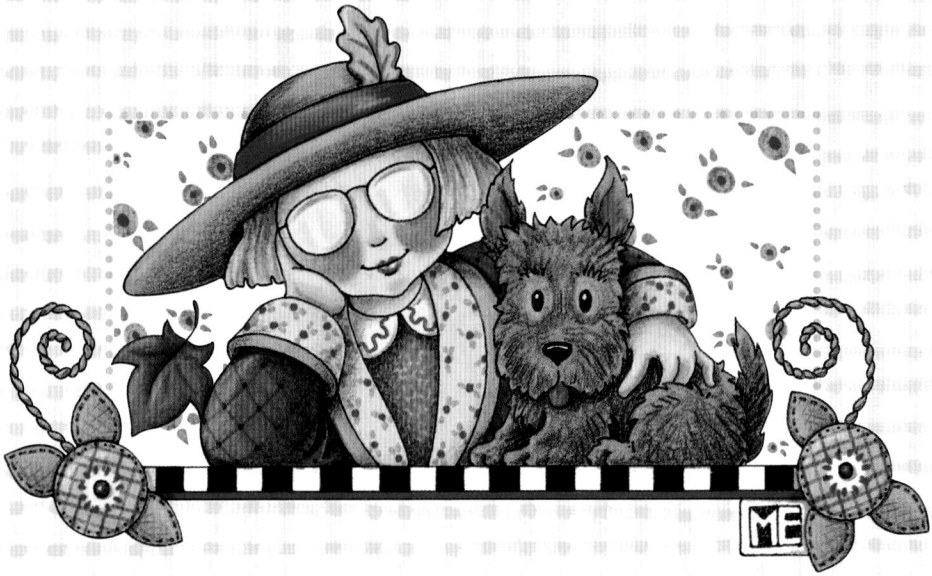

The more I think about it, the more I realize there is nothing more artistic than to love others.

–Vincent van Gogh

...from Mary Engelbreit

In *Words to Live By,* I have put together a collection of drawings that are based on many of my favorite quotations, proverbs, and bits of wisdom. So many of my greeting cards, calendars and drawings illustrate the thoughts and ideas of other people as well as my own.

I grew up reading and still have a huge appetite for literature. Many of my most well known sayings have come from some of my favorite authors. You will find within these pages quotations from all kinds of authors, and the best part is that we all can interpret them in our own way. Graham Greene's comment "there is always one moment in childhood when the door opens and lets the future in," was especially meaningful to me because I wanted to be an artist at a very early age.

I also hear wonderful words to illustrate all around me everyday. Things my children, my friends and their children say often wind up as card images or a calendar page, and I conclude this book with a few of these pieces of wit or wisdom that I have gathered. For example, when I was a girl, my neighbor's slip of the tongue developed into one of my better known sayings, "Life Is Just a Chair of Bowlies." I used this spoonerism to launch my greeting card business twenty years ago. My son, Will, gave me "A Little Peace of Quiet," and my son, Evan, inspired "A Man Among Men," which are, for obvious reasons, two of my favorite drawings.

I hope the readers of this work enjoy these "Words to Live By" as much as I have enjoyed illustrating them.

Mary

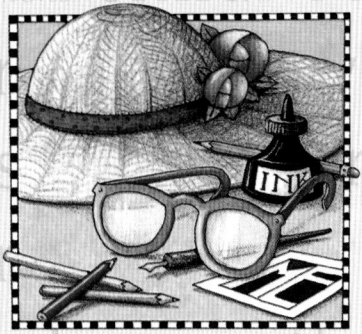
INK

...from great writers

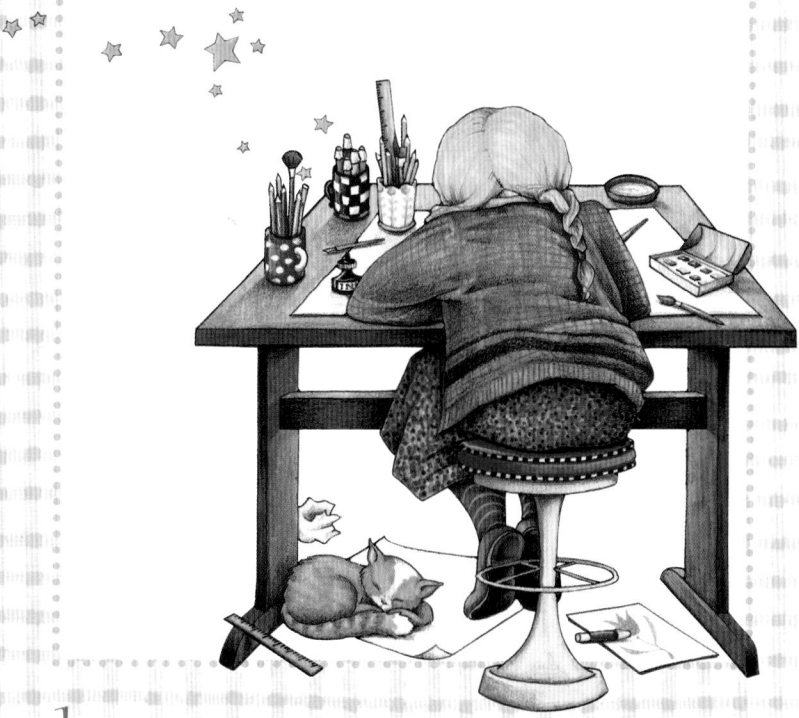

It is art that makes life, makes interest, makes importance, and I know of no substitute for the force and beauty of its process.

–Henry James

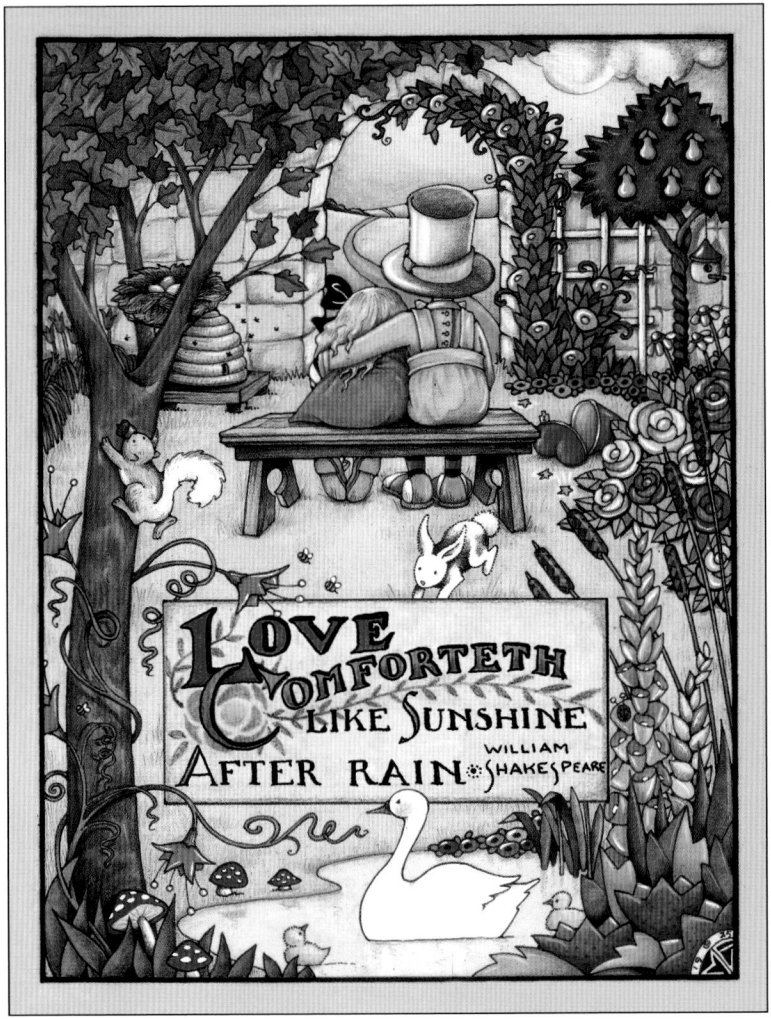
LOVE COMFORTETH LIKE SUNSHINE AFTER RAIN
WILLIAM SHAKESPEARE

Love and you shall be loved.
-Ralph Waldo Emerson

Love is a great beautifier.
-Louisa May Alcott

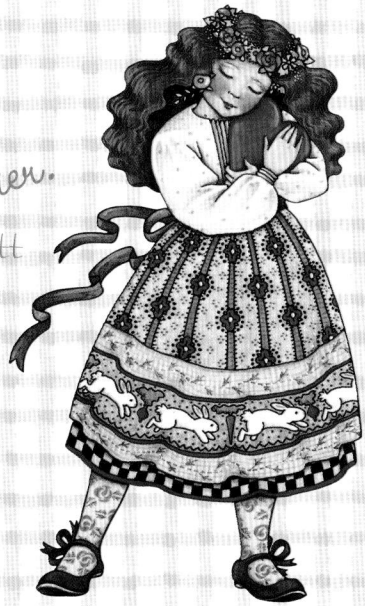

Love conquers all.
-Virgil

Where there is great love,
there are always miracles.
-Willa Cather

But there's nothing
half so sweet in life
as love's young dream.
-Thomas Moore

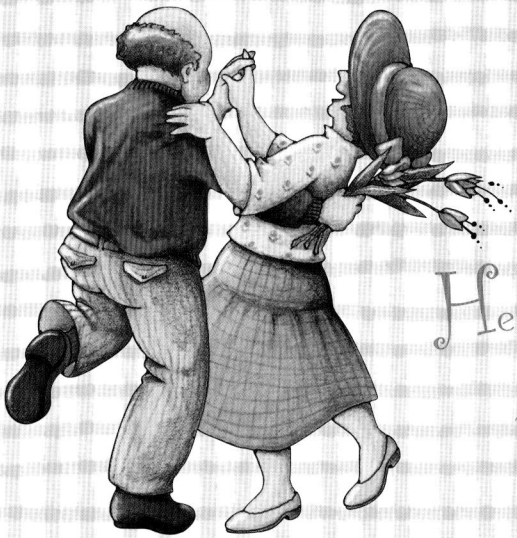

Heaven is under our feet
as well as over our heads.
-Henry David Thoreau

To a young heart everything is fun.
-Charles Dickens

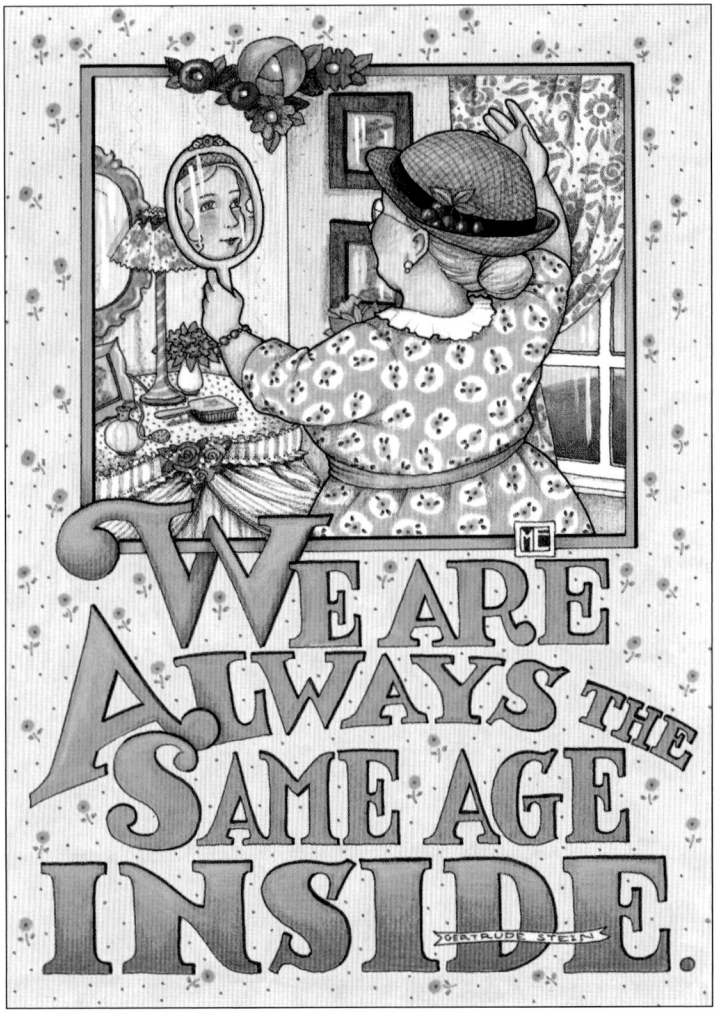
MC
WE ARE ALWAYS THE SAME AGE INSIDE.
GERTRUDE STEIN

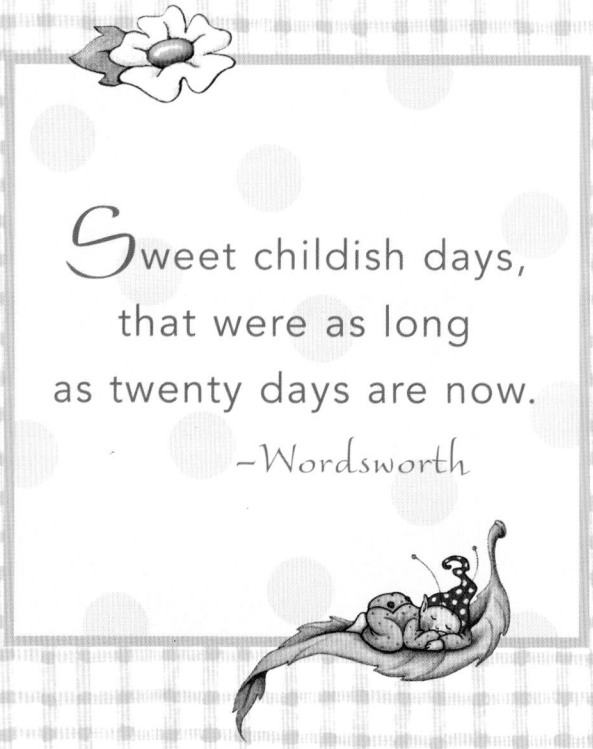
Sweet childish days,
that were as long
as twenty days are now.
–Wordsworth

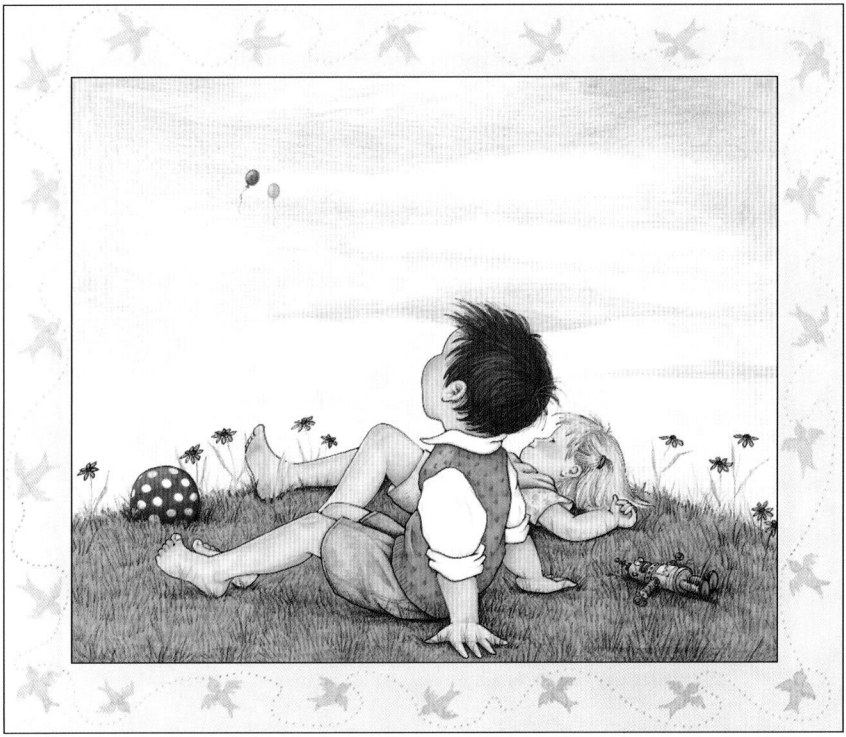

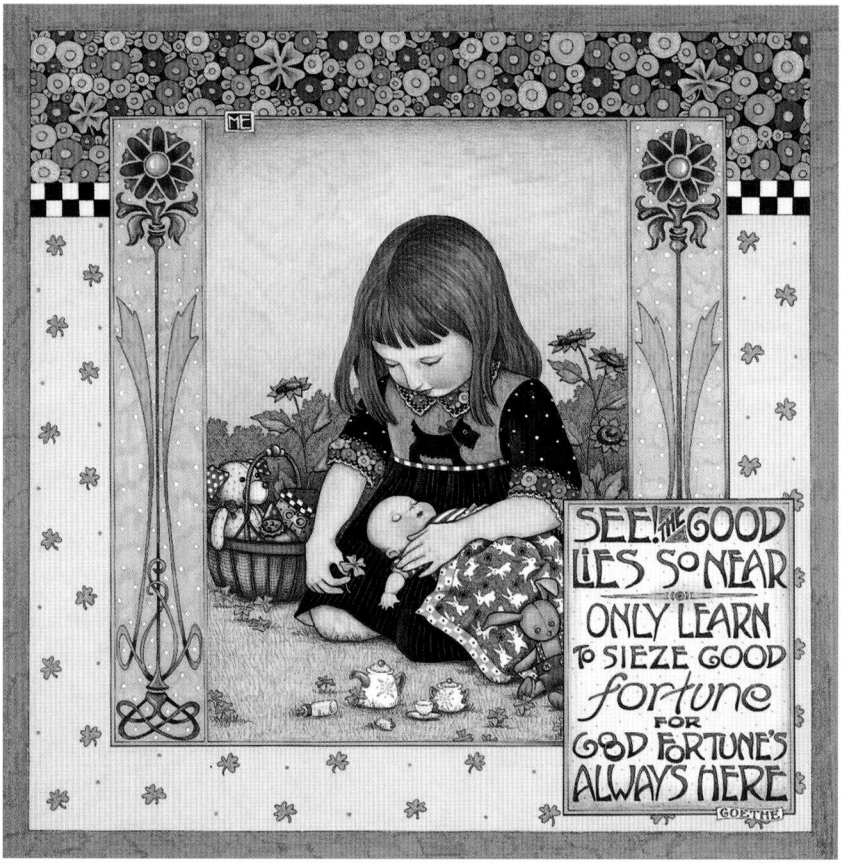
ME
SEE! THE GOOD
LIES SO NEAR
ONLY LEARN
TO SIEZE GOOD
fortune
FOR
GOD FORTUNE'S
ALWAYS HERE
GOETHE

Never lose a chance
of saying a kind word.
–William Makepeace Thackeray

We ought, everyday,
to hear a song,
read a fine poem,
and, if possible,
to speak a few reasonable words.
–Goethe

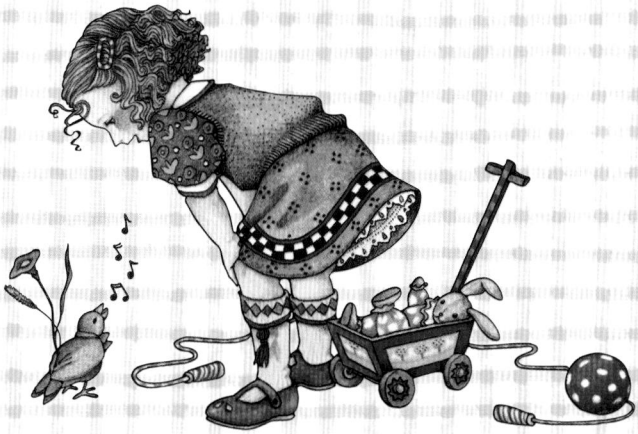

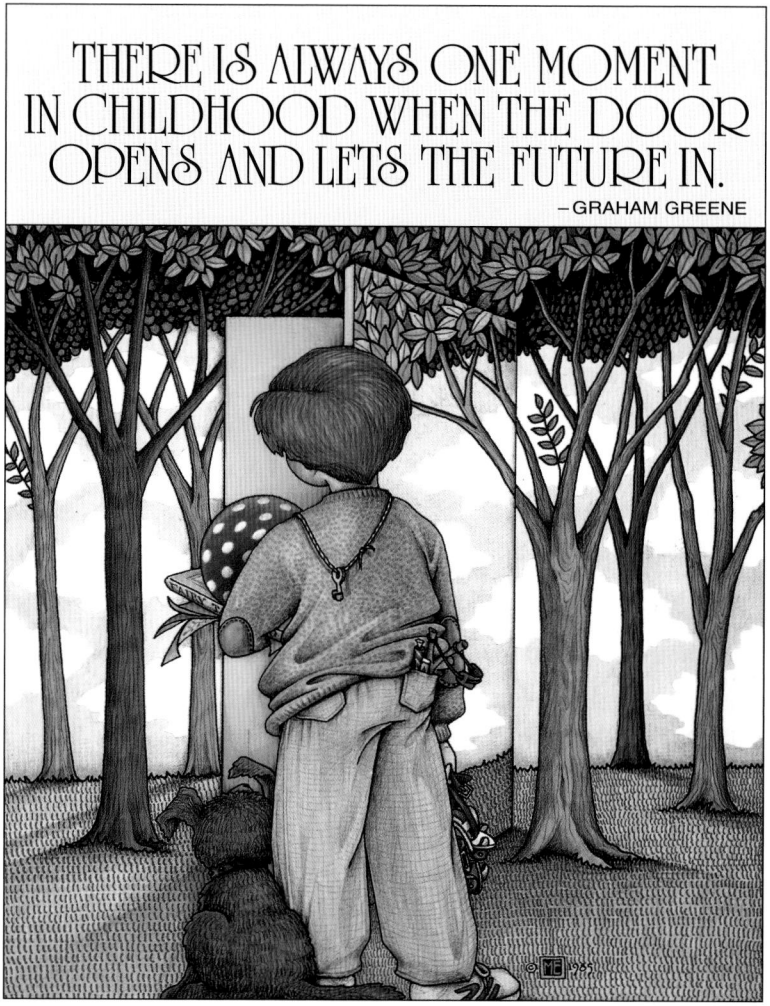
THERE IS ALWAYS ONE MOMENT
IN CHILDHOOD WHEN THE DOOR
OPENS AND LETS THE FUTURE IN.
–GRAHAM GREENE

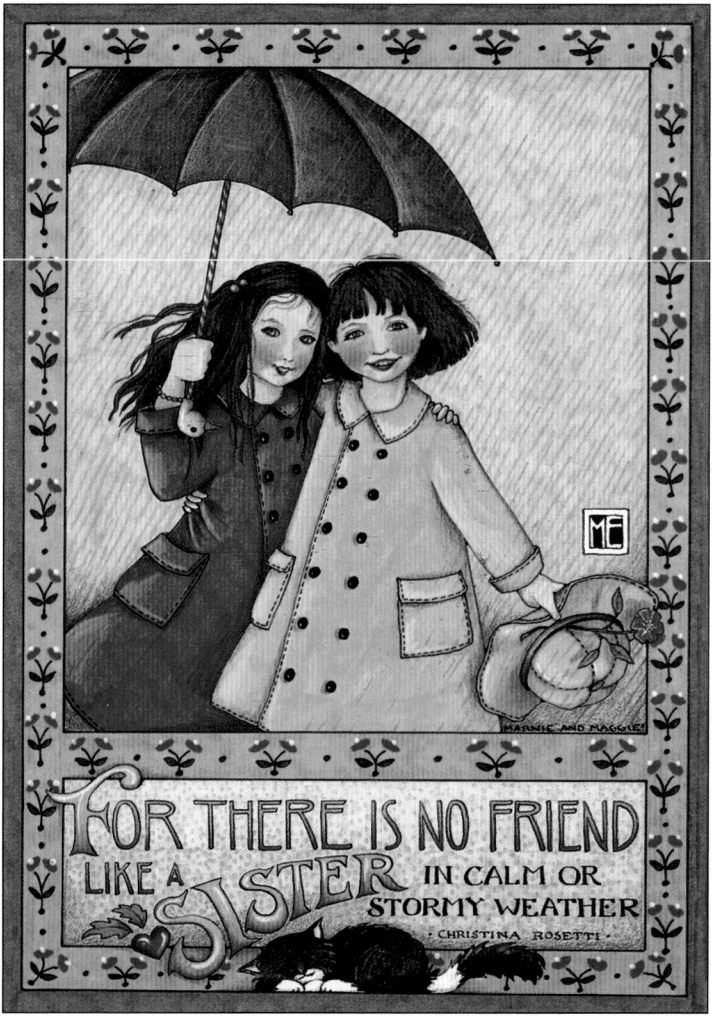
MC
MARNIE AND MAGGIE
FOR THERE IS NO FRIEND
LIKE A SISTER IN CALM OR
STORMY WEATHER
- CHRISTINA ROSETTI -

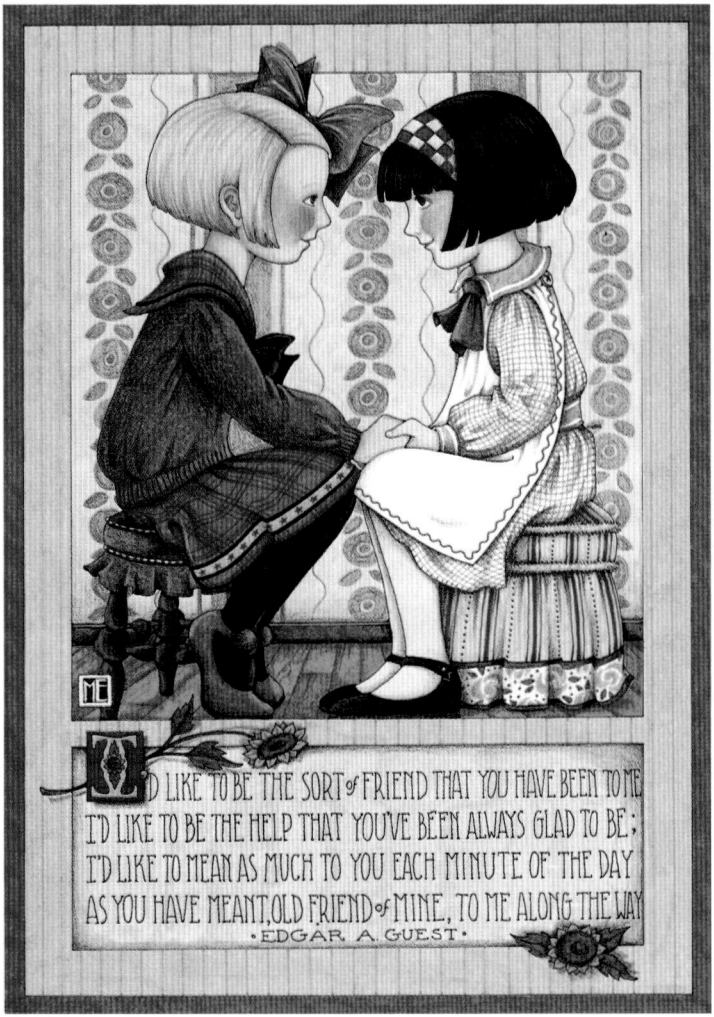
ME
I'D LIKE TO BE THE SORT OF FRIEND THAT YOU HAVE BEEN TO ME;
I'D LIKE TO BE THE HELP THAT YOU'VE BEEN ALWAYS GLAD TO BE;
I'D LIKE TO MEAN AS MUCH TO YOU EACH MINUTE OF THE DAY
AS YOU HAVE MEANT, OLD FRIEND OF MINE, TO ME ALONG THE WAY
• EDGAR A. GUEST •

My friends are my estate.
–Emily Dickinson

Friendship is love without wings.
–Lord Byron

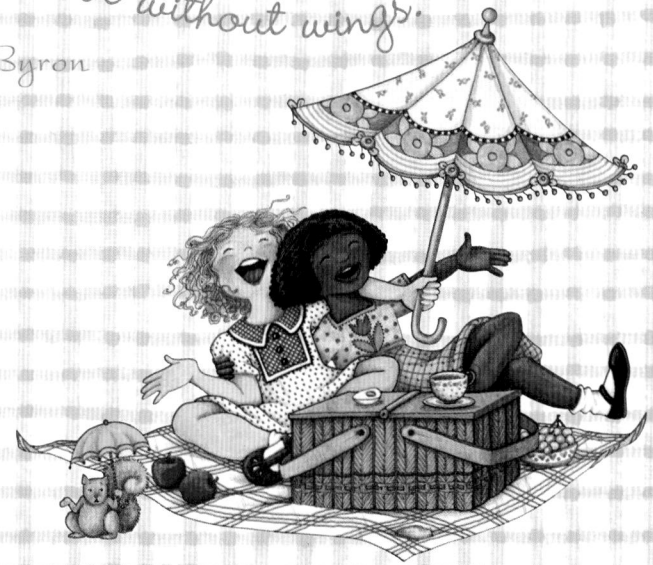

flowers are lovely;
love is flower-like;
Friendship is a sheltering tree.
–Coleridge

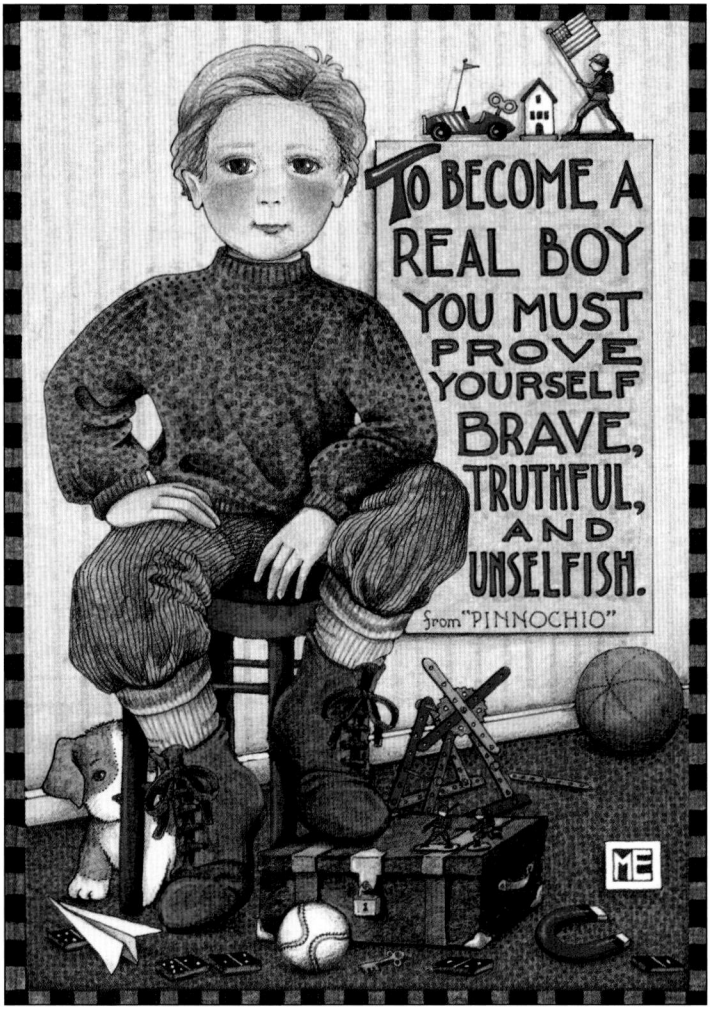
TO BECOME A
REAL BOY
YOU MUST
PROVE
YOURSELF
BRAVE,
TRUTHFUL,
AND
UNSELFISH.
from "PINNOCHIO"
ME

Summer afternoon,
summer afternoon;
to me those have always been
the two most beautiful words
in the english language.

—Henry James

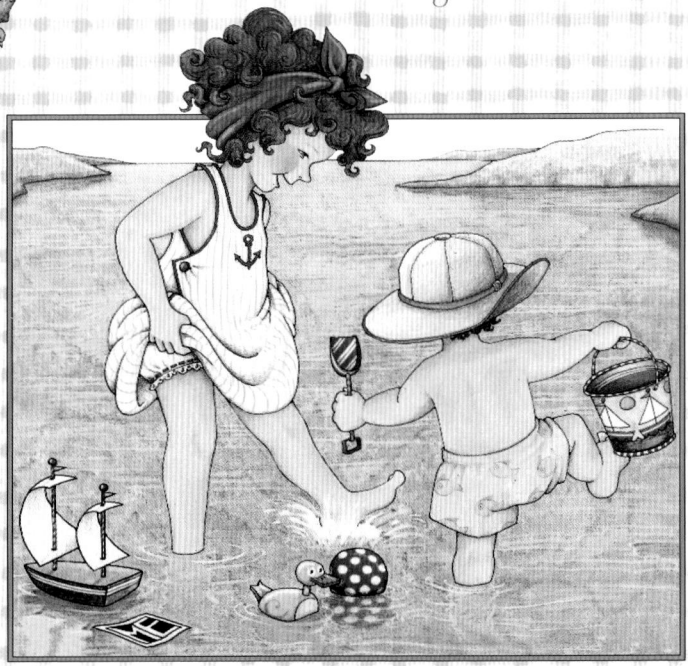

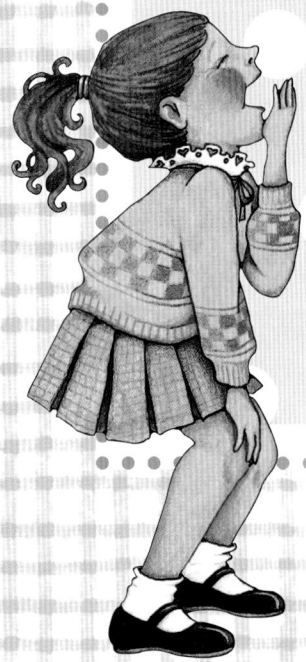

A good laugh is sunshine in a house.

–William Makepeace Thackeray

Keep true to the dreams of your youth.

–Johann Friedrich von Schiller

There is nothing like a dream
to create the future.
–Victor Hugo

The best way to make children good
is to make them happy.
–Oscar Wilde

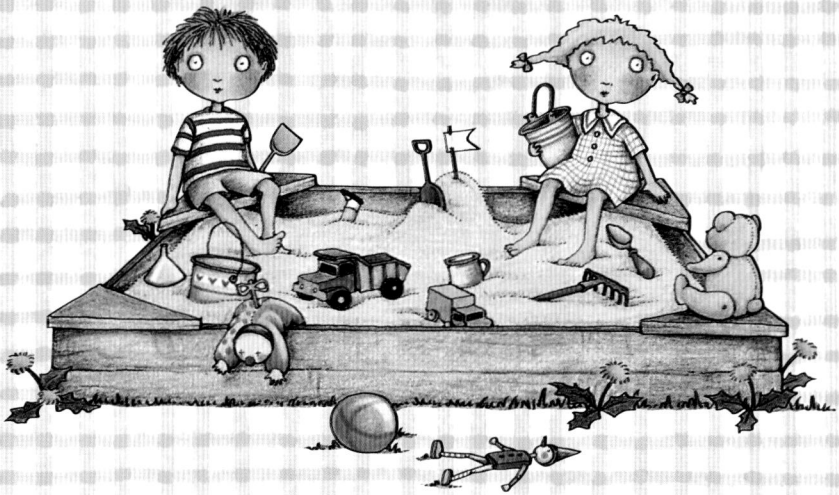

Youth comes but once in a lifetime.
–Henry Wadsworth Longfellow

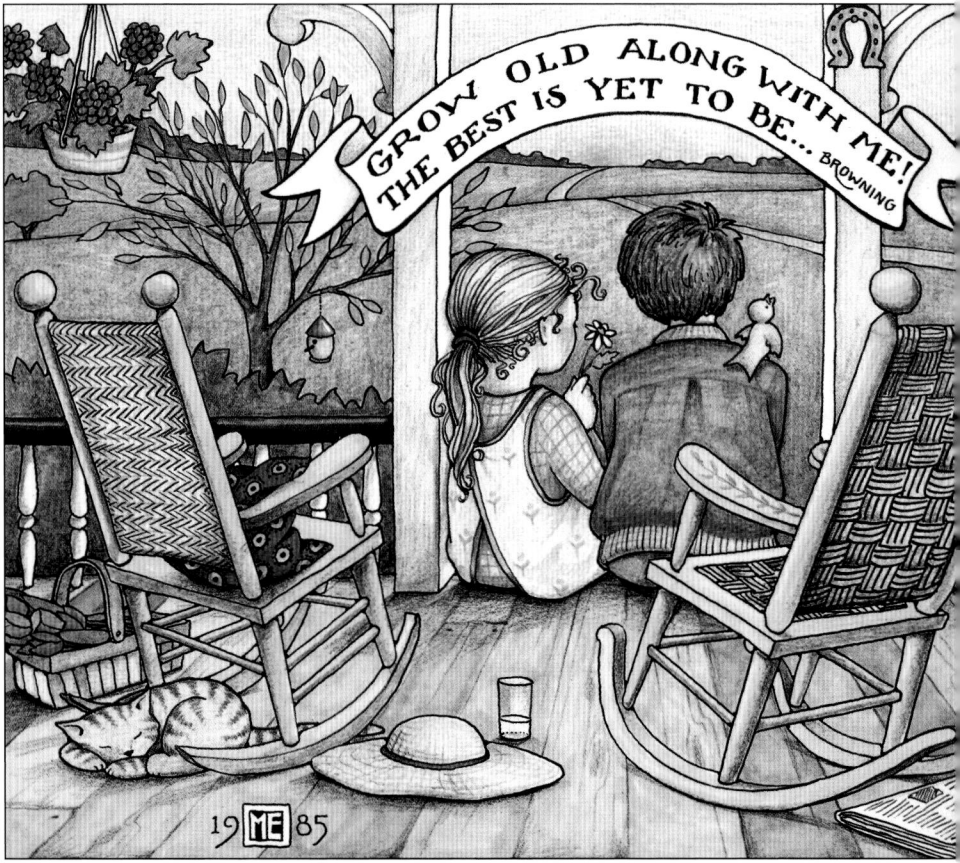
GROW OLD ALONG WITH ME!
THE BEST IS YET TO BE... BROWNING
19 ME 85

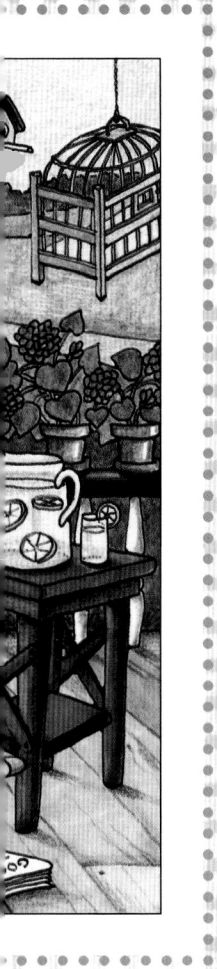

In three words
I can sum up everything I've learned
about life: It goes on.
—Robert Frost

an act of goodness surpasses a thousan
prayers sa 'di do all things with lov
og mandino the heart of the giver make
the gift dear and precious luther eac
has a direction to w ch he turns
so strive to ost in goo
deeds benjamin di there is lov
there is life n on't forget t
love yourself sören kier gaard love is th
river of life in the world henry ward beech
we shall light a candle of unde
standing that shall not be put ou
anonymous make of yourself a light budd
how good and how pleasant it
that brothers sit together

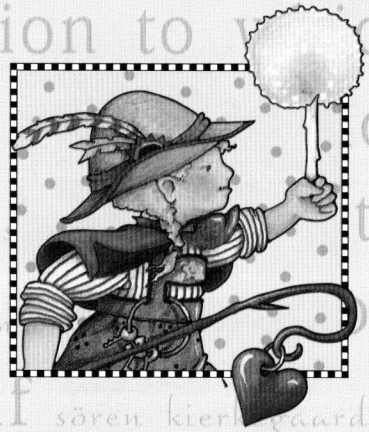

...from great spiritual guides

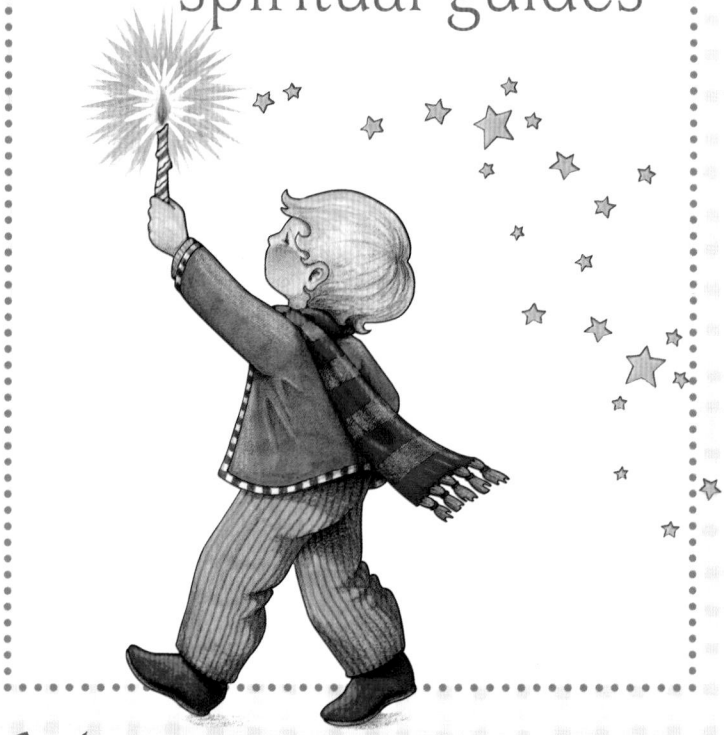

We shall light a candle of understanding in our hearts which shall not be put out.

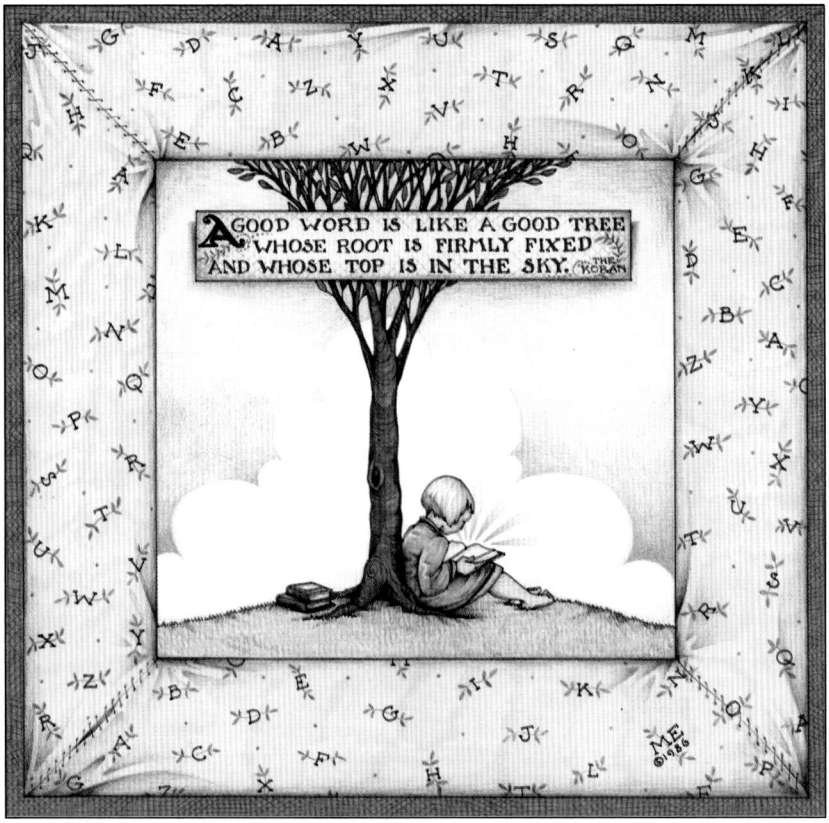
A GOOD WORD IS LIKE A GOOD TREE
WHOSE ROOT IS FIRMLY FIXED
AND WHOSE TOP IS IN THE SKY.
THE KORAN
ME
©1986

Our first teacher is our own heart.

–Cheyenne

Be kind to everything that lives.

–Omaha

An act of goodness surpasses a thousand prayers.

–Sa'di

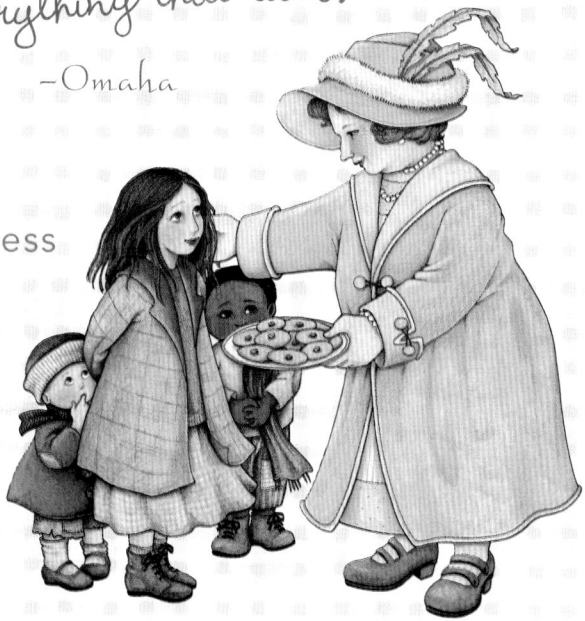

Do all things with love.

–Og Mandino

Where there is love
there is life.
–Mahatma Gandhi

Love is the river of life
in the world.
–Henry Ward Beecher

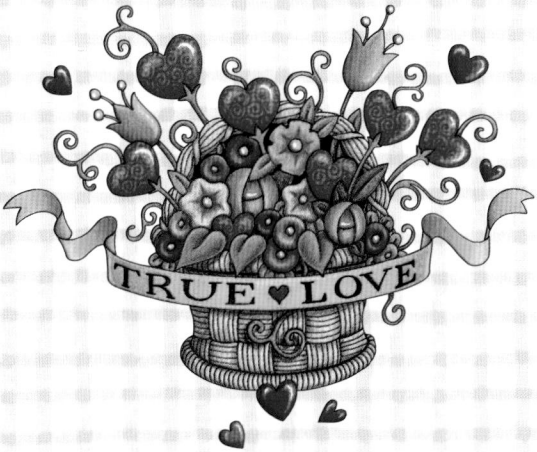

Don't forget to love yourself.
–Sören Kierkegaard

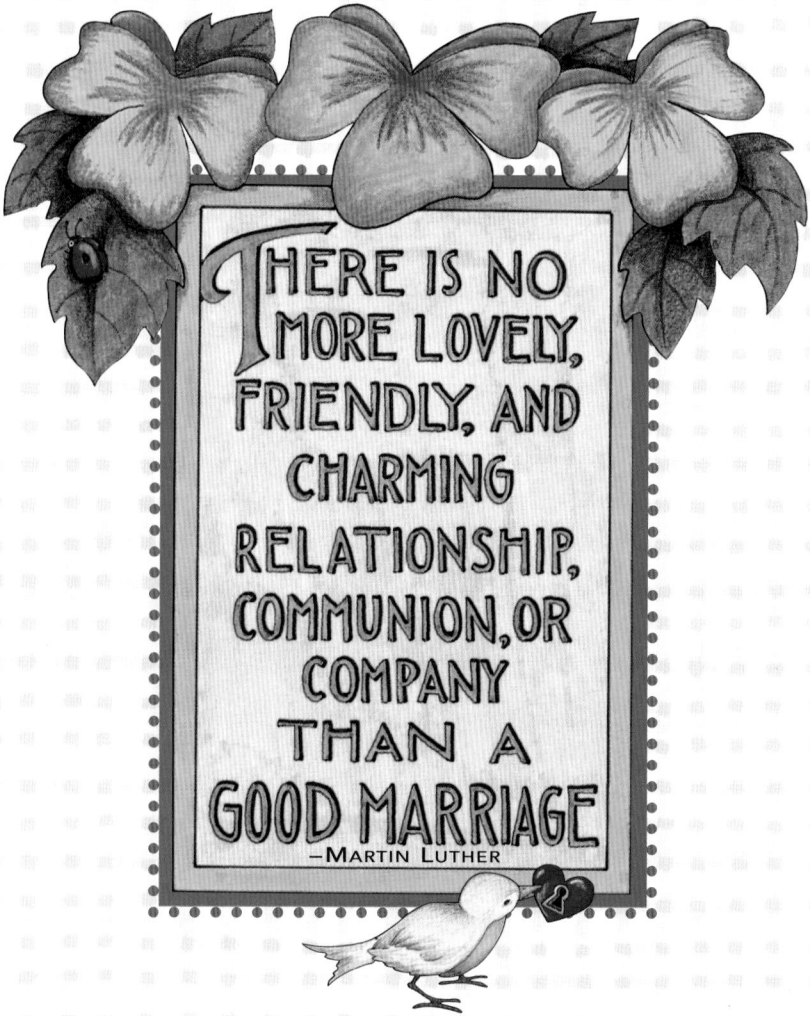
THERE IS NO MORE LOVELY, FRIENDLY, AND CHARMING RELATIONSHIP, COMMUNION, OR COMPANY THAN A GOOD MARRIAGE
—MARTIN LUTHER

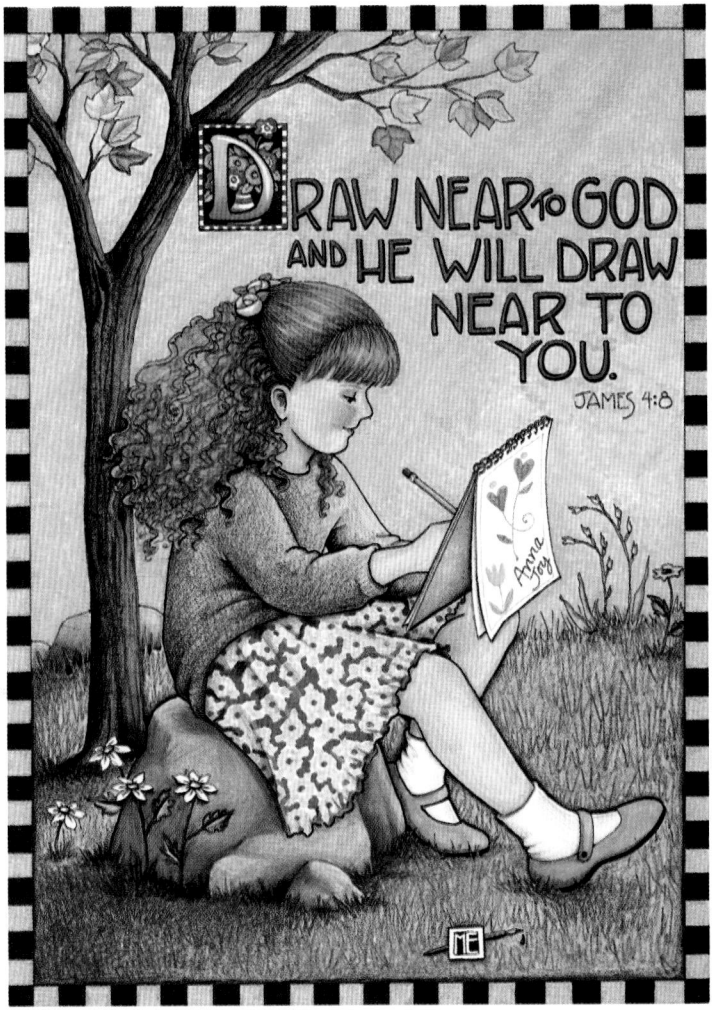
DRAW NEAR TO GOD
AND HE WILL DRAW
NEAR TO
YOU.
JAMES 4:8
Anne Joy
ME

There is no friendship, no love,
like that of the parent
for the child.

–Henry Ward Beecher

How good and how pleasant
it is that brothers sit together.

–Psalm 133:1

A mother's heart
is a child's classroom.

–Henry Ward Beecher

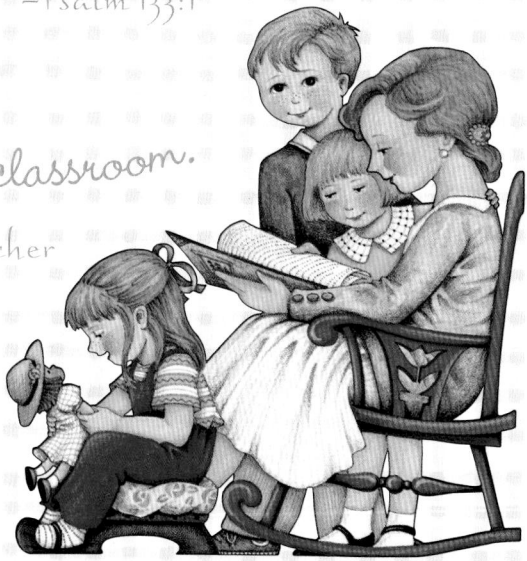

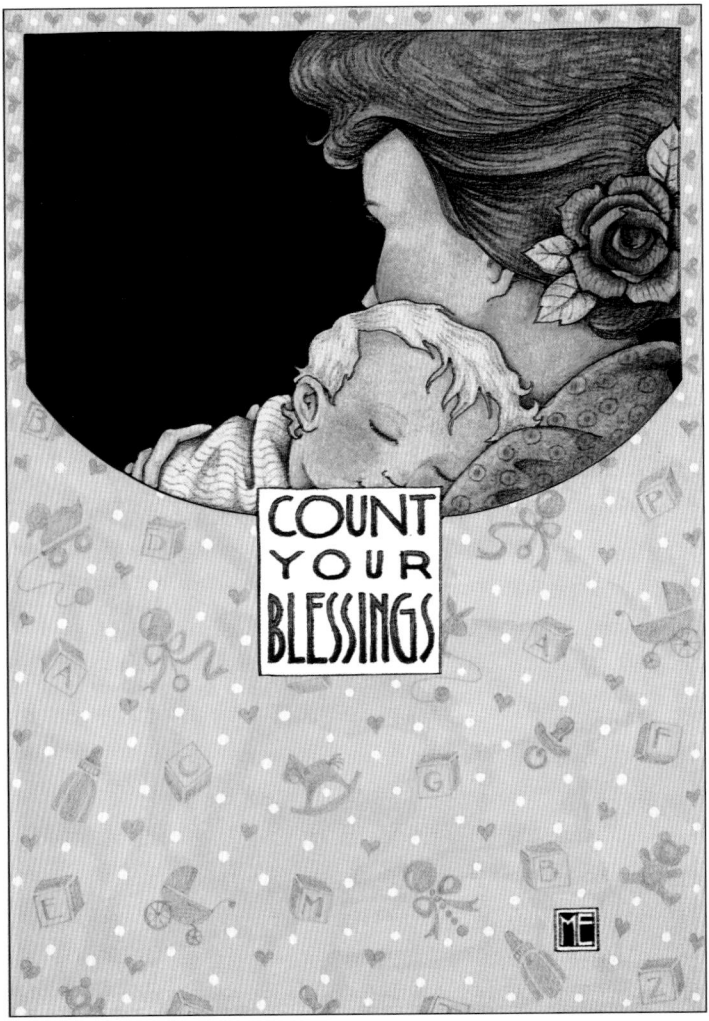
COUNT
YOUR
BLESSINGS
ME

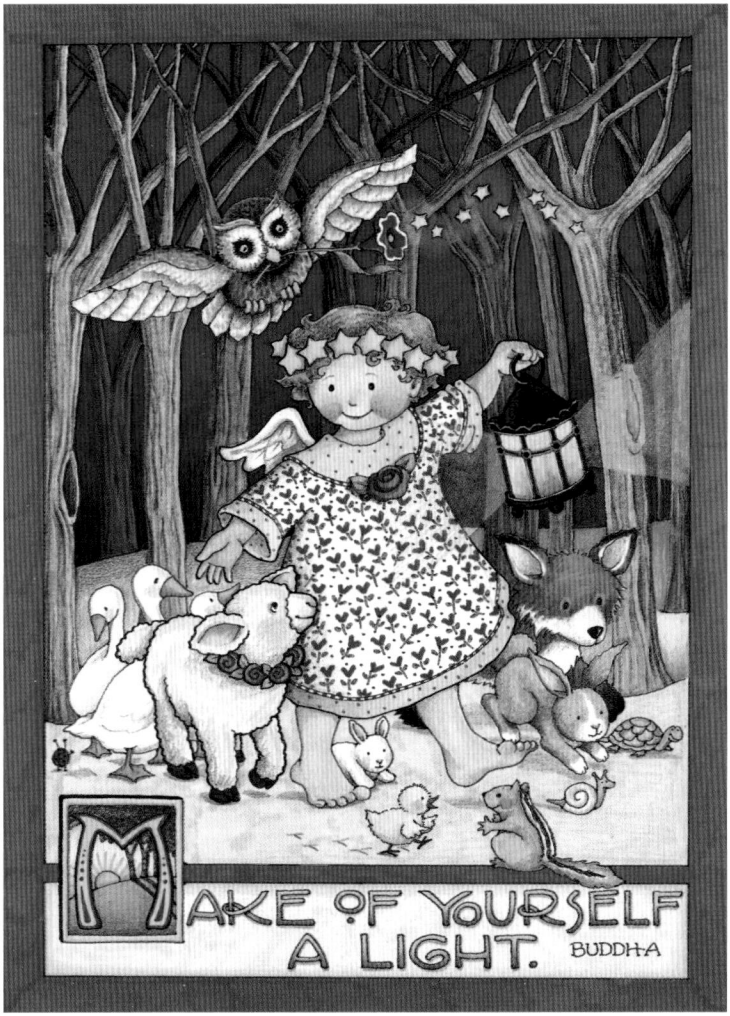
MAKE OF YOURSELF
A LIGHT.
BUDDHA

Each has a direction to which he turns;
so strive to be foremost in good deeds.
–the Koran

The heart of the giver
makes the gift dear and precious.
–Luther

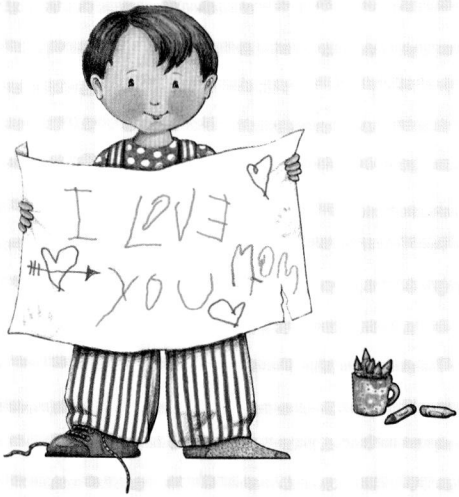

Life is both giving and receiving.
–Mohawk

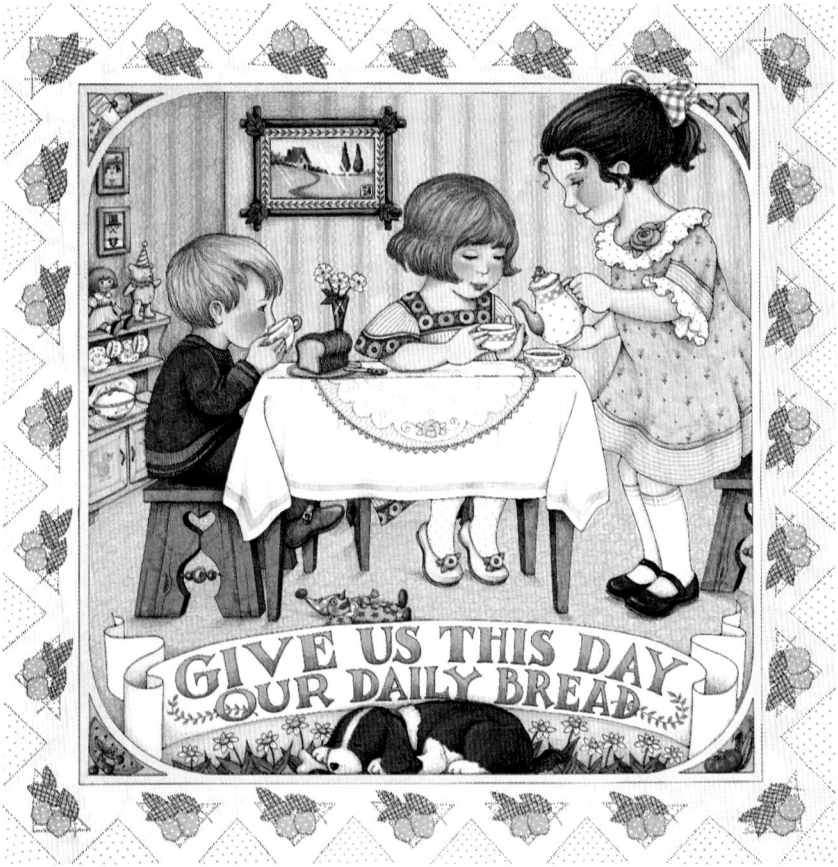
GIVE US THIS DAY
OUR DAILY BREAD

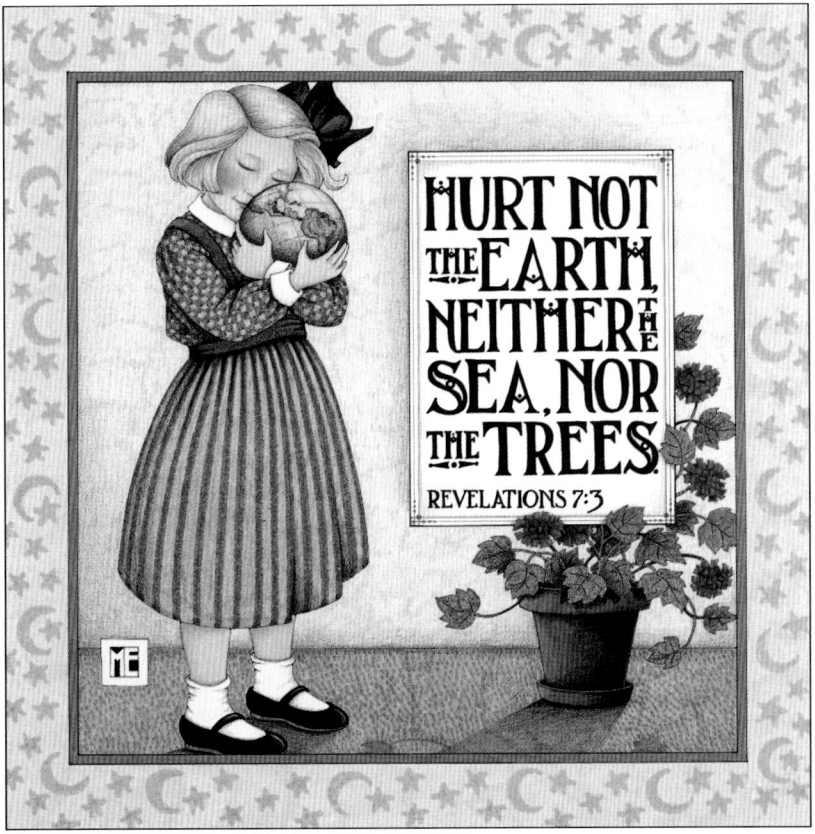
HURT NOT
THE EARTH,
NEITHER THE
SEA, NOR
THE TREES.
REVELATIONS 7:3
ME

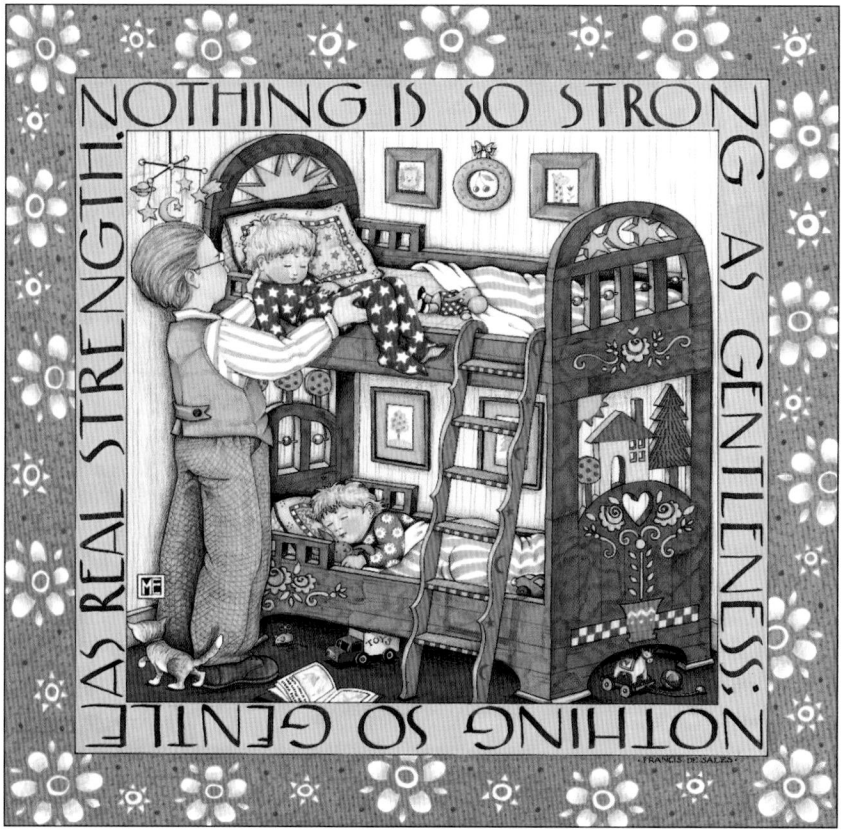
NOTHING IS SO STRONG AS GENTLENESS, NOTHING SO GENTLE AS REAL STRENGTH.
TOYS
«FRANCIS DE SALES»

only from the heart can you touc
the sky rumi all great things are simpl
ir winston churchill in all things of natur
there is something of the marvelou
ristotle no act of kindness, no matte
now small, is ed aesop to loo
up is joy con on, there i
strength aesop w ns in wonde
ocrates we make living by what w
get, but we make a life by what w
give sir winston churchill a true friend is th
best possession benjamin franklin our lif
s what our thoughts make it marc
urelius the future belongs to those wh
believe in the beauty of their dream

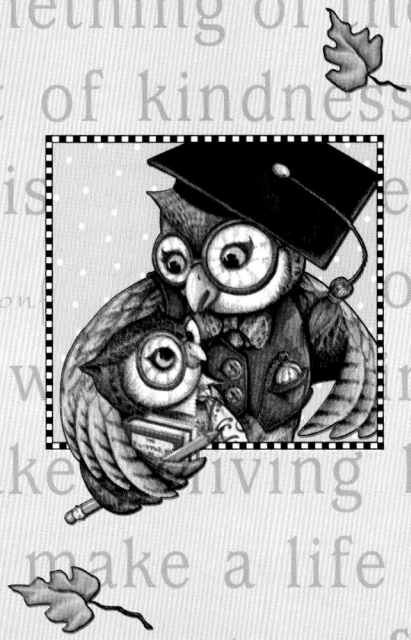

...from great thinkers

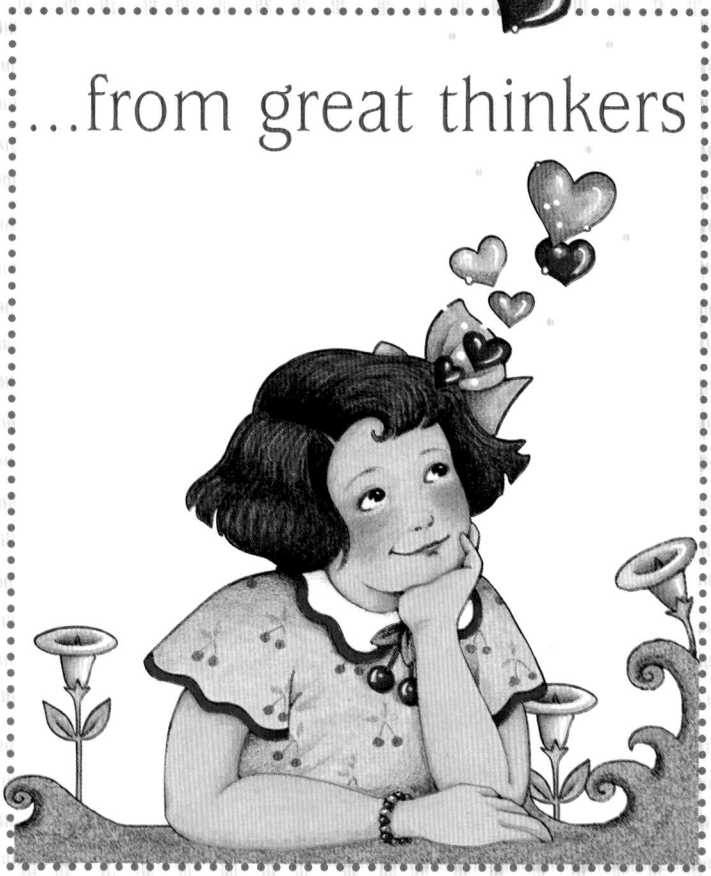

Nurture your mind with great thoughts.

–Benjamin Disraeli

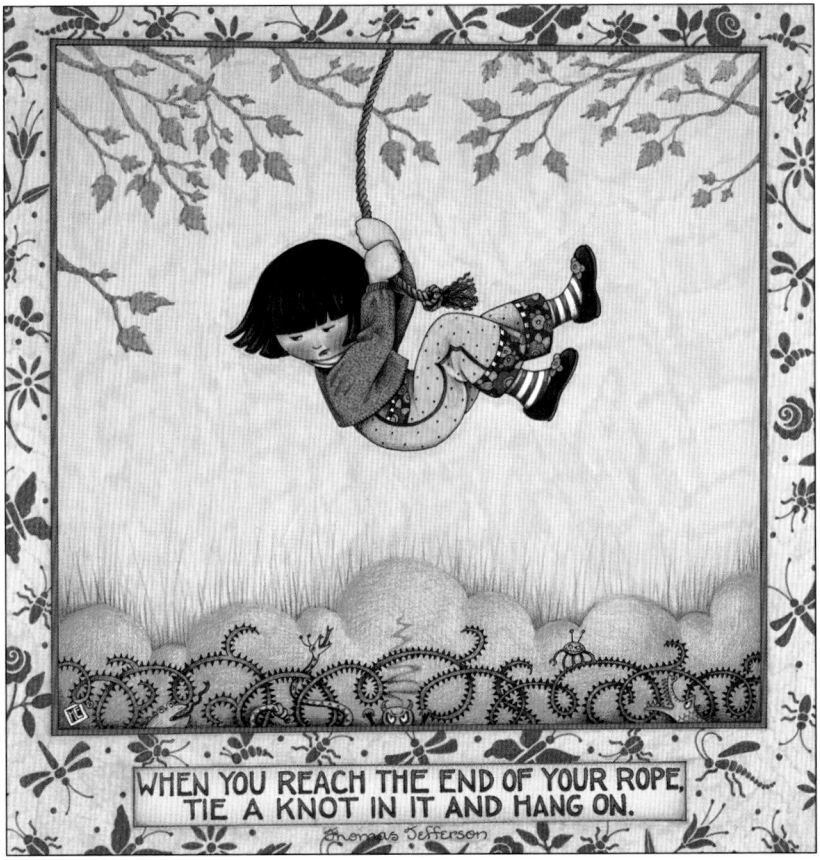
WHEN YOU REACH THE END OF YOUR ROPE,
TIE A KNOT IN IT AND HANG ON.
Thomas Jefferson

The highest form of bliss
is living with
a certain degree of folly.
–Erasmus

To live is to function.
That is all there is in living.
–Oliver Wendell Holmes

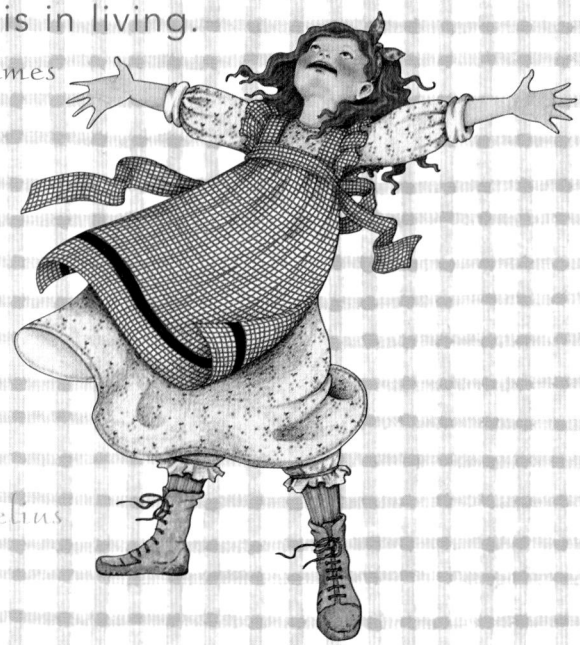

Remember that
very little is needed
to make a happy life.
–Marcus Aurelius

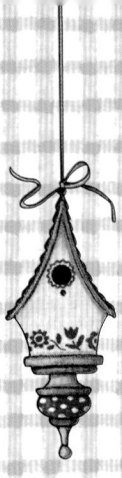

The best thing about the future
is that it comes only
one day at a time.
—Abraham Lincoln

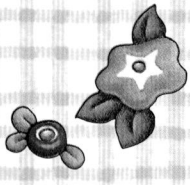

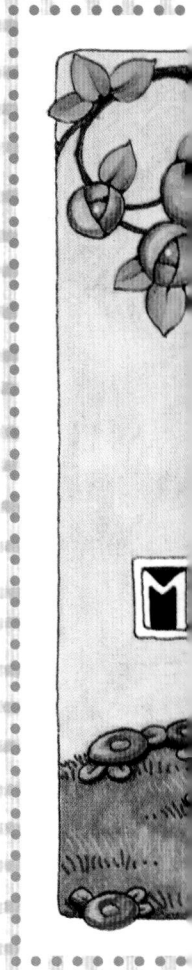

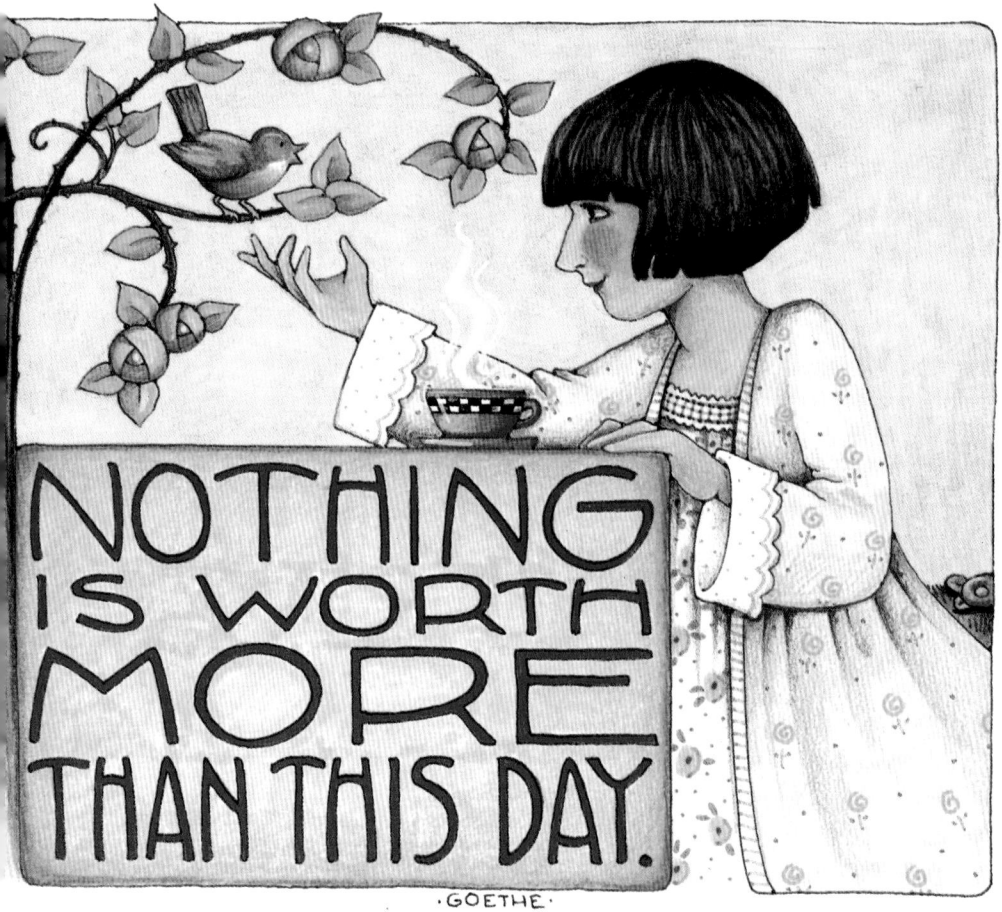
NOTHING
IS WORTH
MORE
THAN THIS DAY.
·GOETHE·

A short saying
often contains much wisdom.
–Sophocles

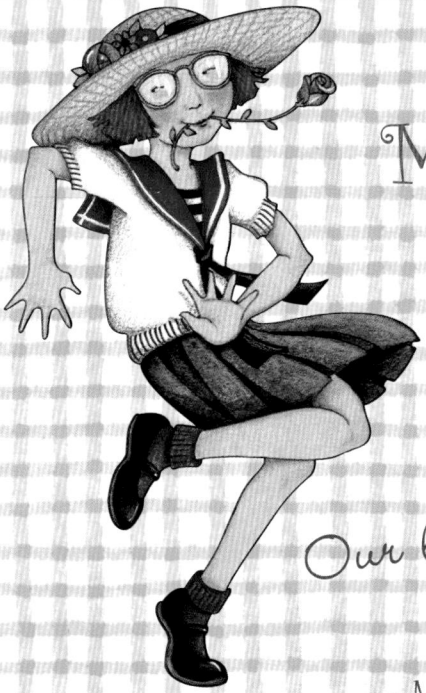

Most folks
are about as happy
as they make up
their minds to be.
–Abraham Lincoln

Our life is what
our thoughts make it.
–Marcus Aurelius

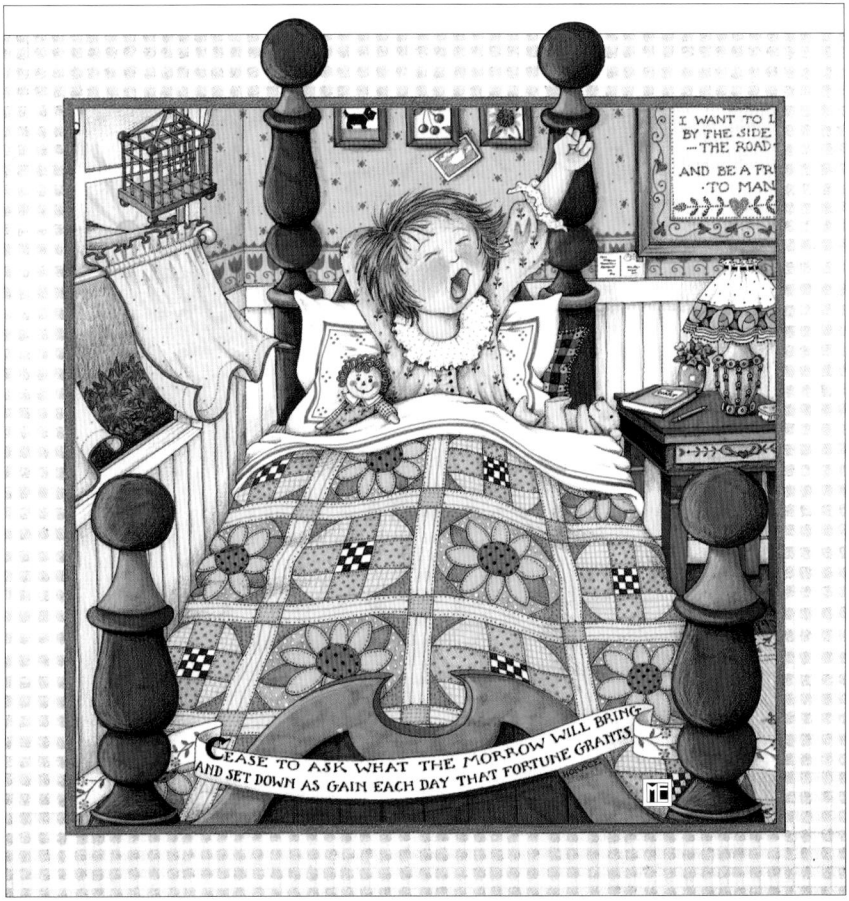
I WANT TO L
BY THE SIDE
— THE ROAD
AND BE A FR
TO MAN
CEASE TO ASK WHAT THE MORROW WILL BRING
AND SET DOWN AS GAIN EACH DAY THAT FORTUNE GRANTS
HORACE

The happiest moments of my life
have been the few which I have passed at home
in the bosom of my family.
–Thomas Jefferson

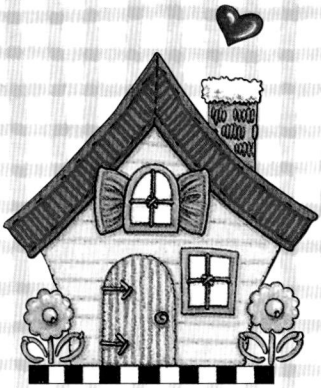

Where we love is home.
Home that our feet may leave
but not our hearts.
–Oliver Wendell Holmes

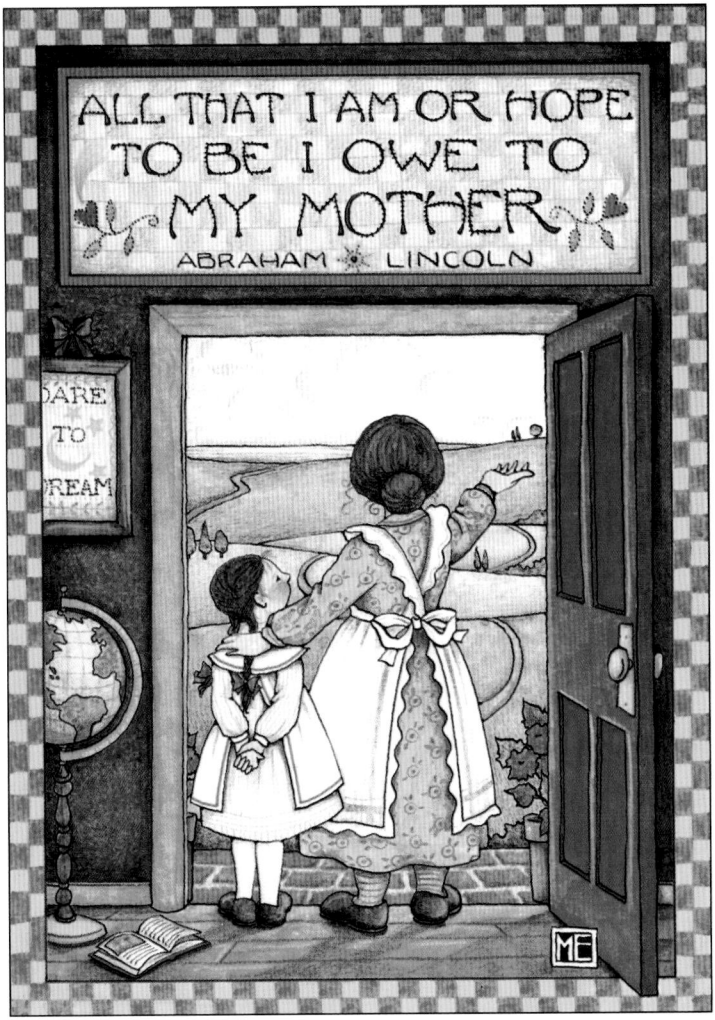
ALL THAT I AM OR HOPE
TO BE I OWE TO
MY MOTHER
ABRAHAM LINCOLN
ARE
TO
REAM
MC

In union,
there is strength.
—Aesop

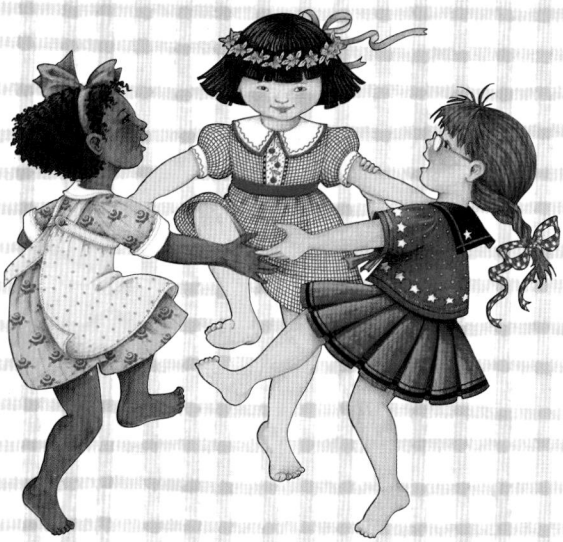

A true friend is the best possession.
—Benjamin Franklin

Friendship is the only cement
that will ever hold the world together.
—Woodrow Wilson

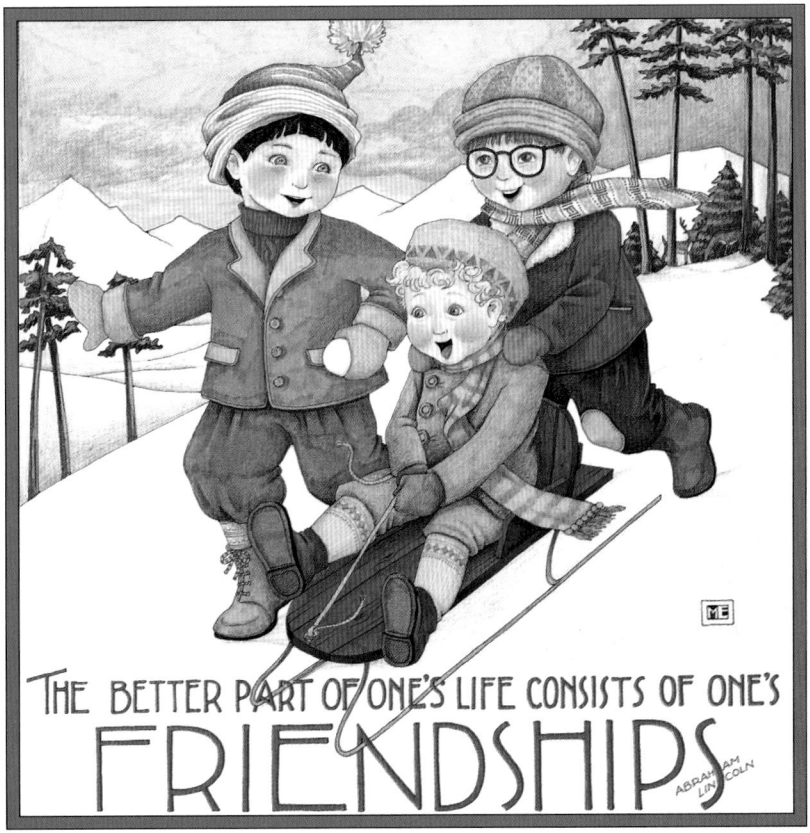
THE BETTER PART OF ONE'S LIFE CONSISTS OF ONE'S
FRIENDSHIPS
ABRAHAM LINCOLN

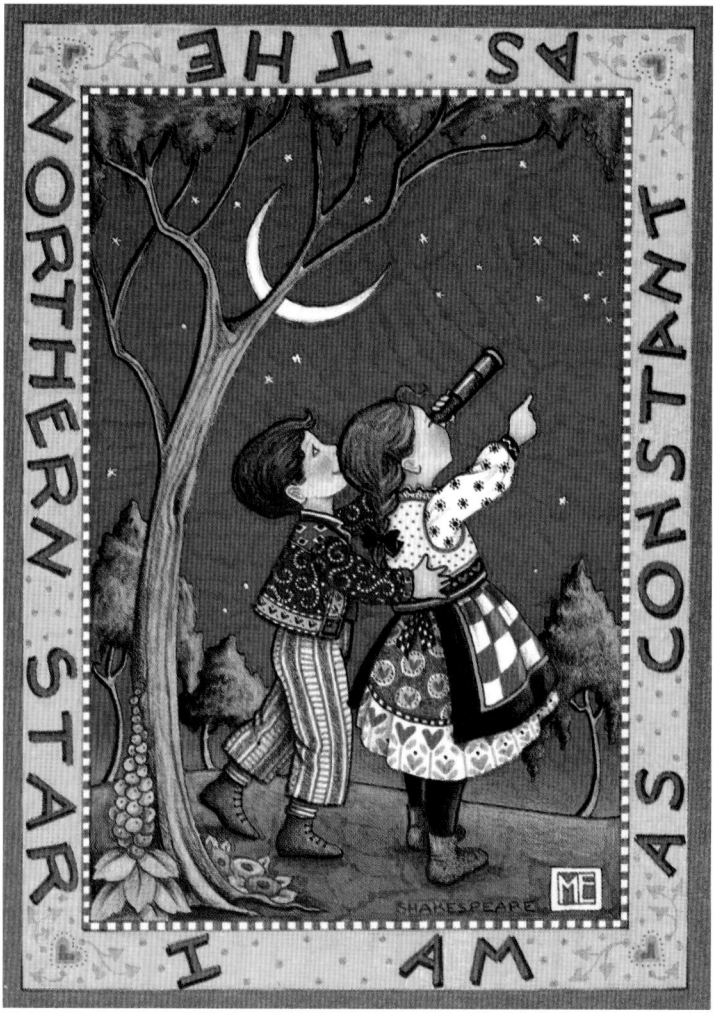
I AM AS CONSTANT AS THE NORTHERN STAR
SHAKESPEARE
ME

The future belongs to those
who believe in the beauty
of their dreams.
—Eleanor Roosevelt

To look up is joy.
—Confucius

Only from the heart
can you touch the sky.
—Rumi

Wisdom begins in wonder.
—Socrates

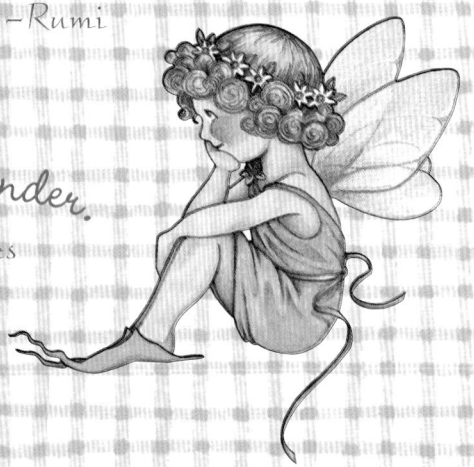

No act of kindness,
no matter how small, is ever wasted.
–Aesop

All the great things
are simple.
–Sir Winston Churchill

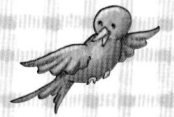

In all things of nature there
is something of the marvelous.
–Aristotle

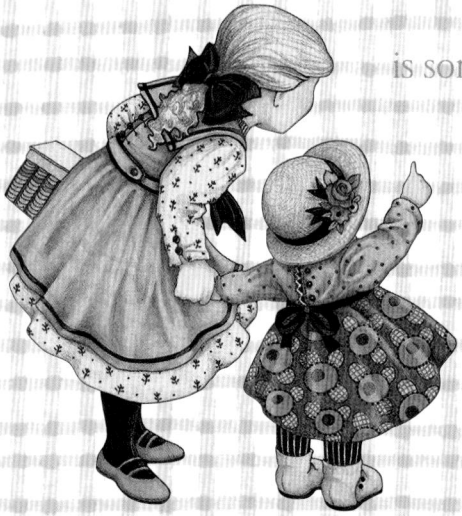

We make a living
by what we get,
but we make a life
by what we give.
–Sir Winston Churchill

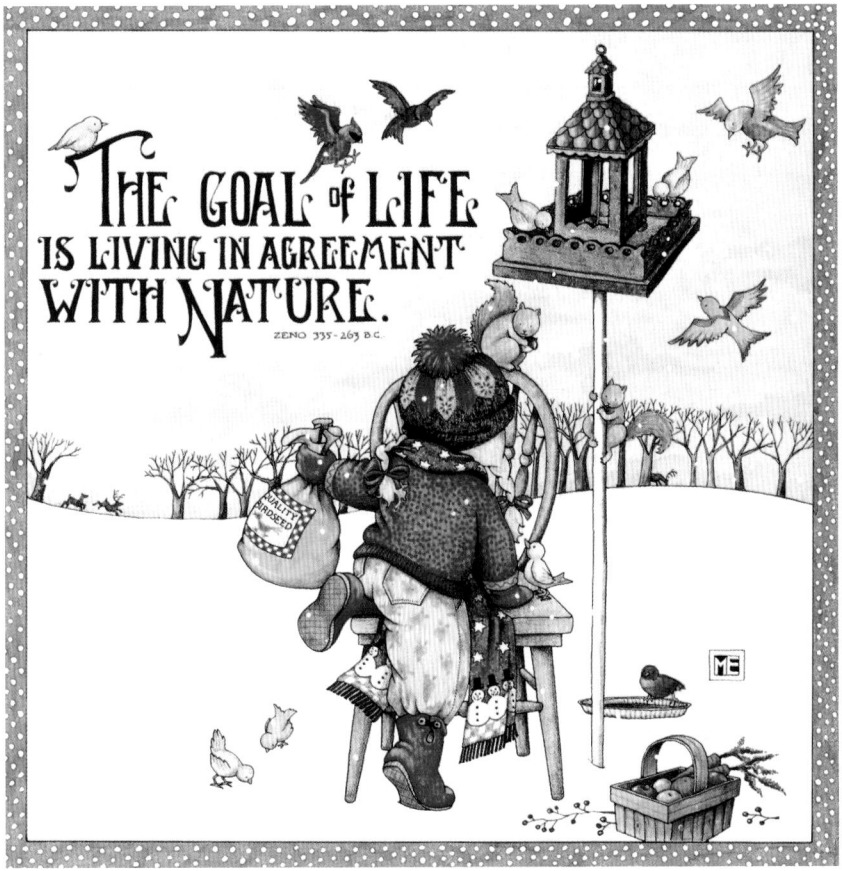
THE GOAL OF LIFE
IS LIVING IN AGREEMENT
WITH NATURE.
ZENO 335-263 B.C.
MALLEE PRODUCTS
ME

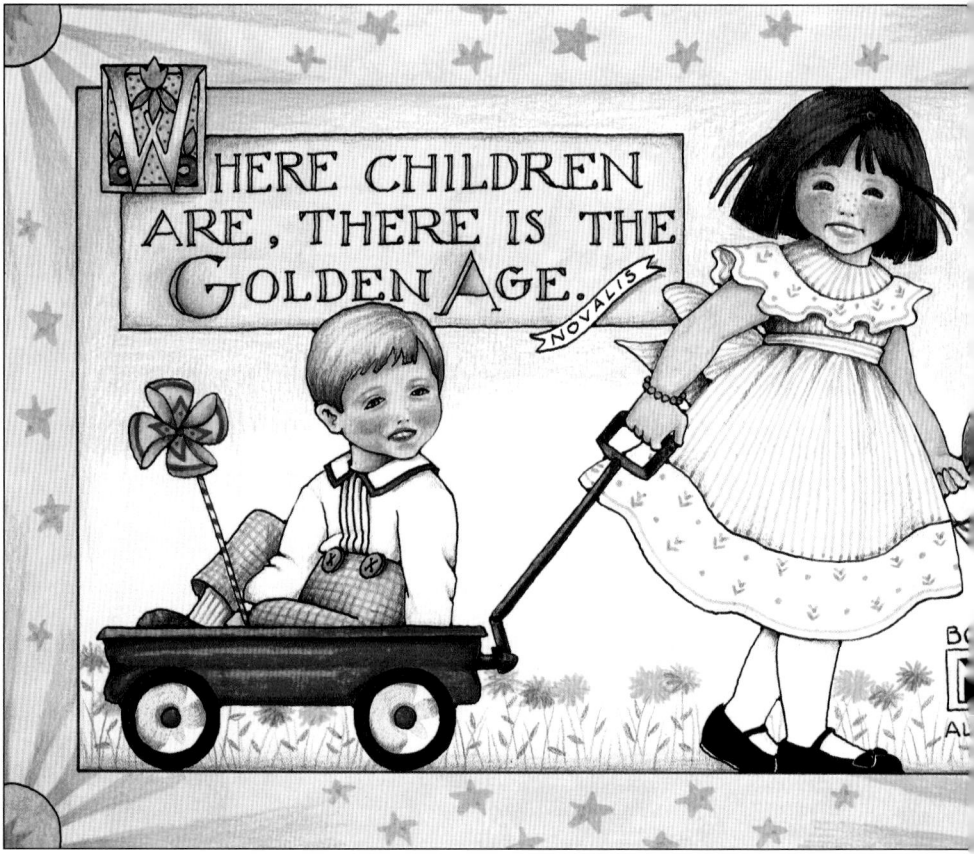
WHERE CHILDREN ARE, THERE IS THE GOLDEN AGE.
NOVALIS

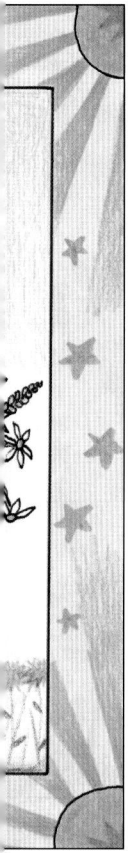

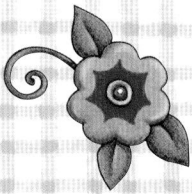

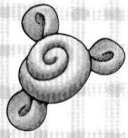

Seek the wisdom
of the ages,
but look at the world
through the eyes of a child.
–Anonymous

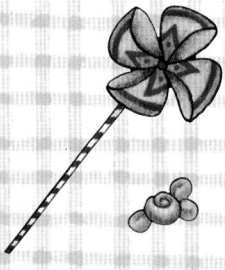

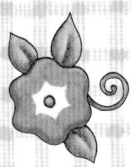

happiness is made to be shared fren

roverb bricks and mortar make a hous

out the laughter of children makes

home irish proverb who takes the child b

the hand takes the mother by th

heart danish prover ild is born, s

s a grandmot when ther

s room in t here is roor

n the house danish proverb keep compan

with those who make you better engli

aging the heart that loves is alway

young greek proverb a life without a frien

s a life without sun french proverb we hav

not inherited the earth from ou

fathers, we are borrowing it from ou

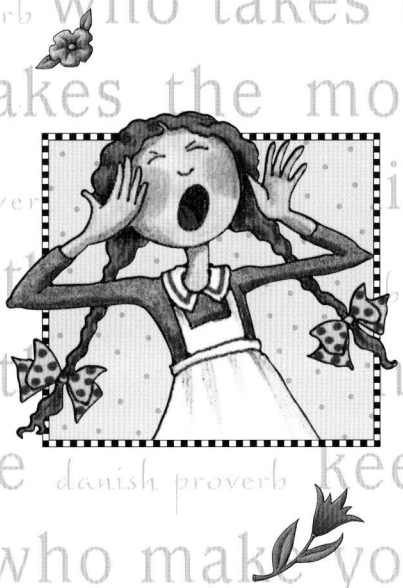

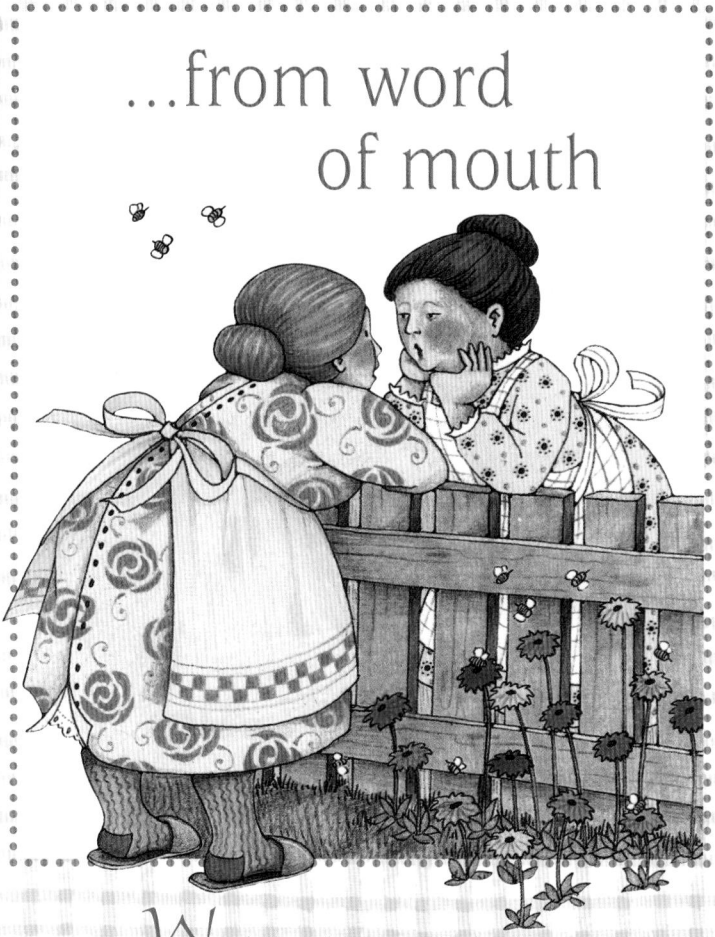

Words are the voice of the heart.

—Confucius

To believe everything is too much,
to believe nothing
is not enough.
–German proverb

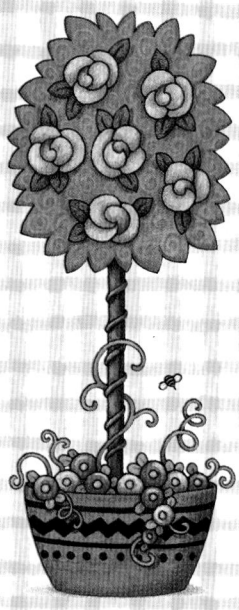

It is by believing
in roses
that one brings
them to bloom.
–French proverb

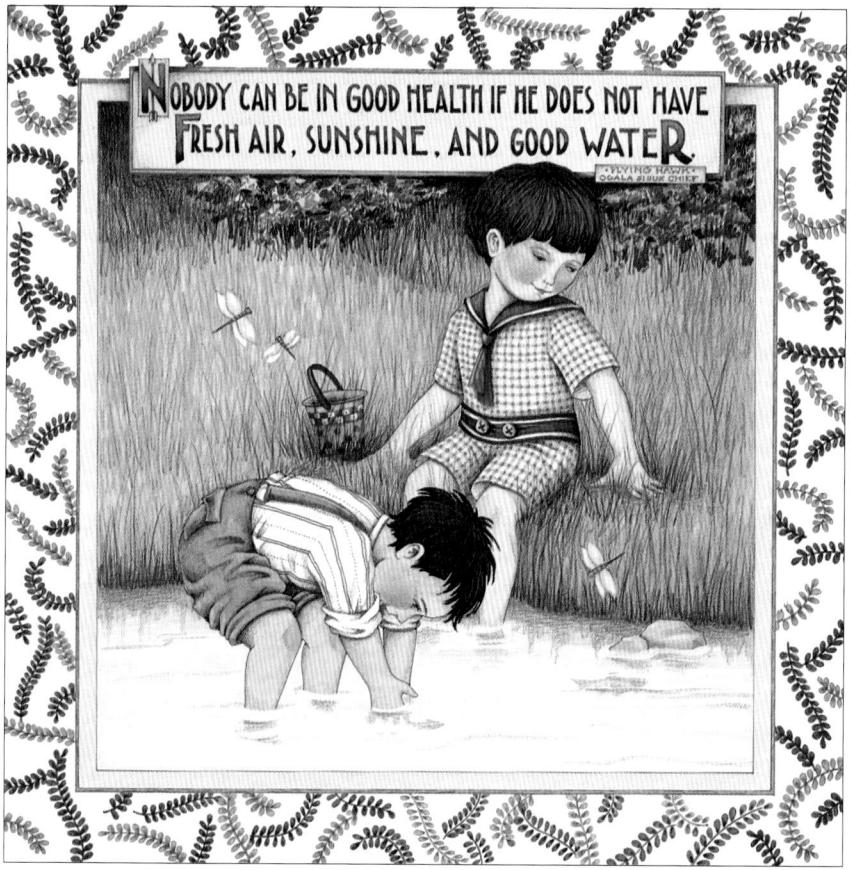
NOBODY CAN BE IN GOOD HEALTH IF HE DOES NOT HAVE
FRESH AIR, SUNSHINE, AND GOOD WATER
-FLYING HAWK
OGALA SIOUX CHIEF

Bricks and mortar make a house
but the laughter of children
makes a home.

–Irish proverb

When there is
room in the heart,
there is room in the house.

–Danish proverb

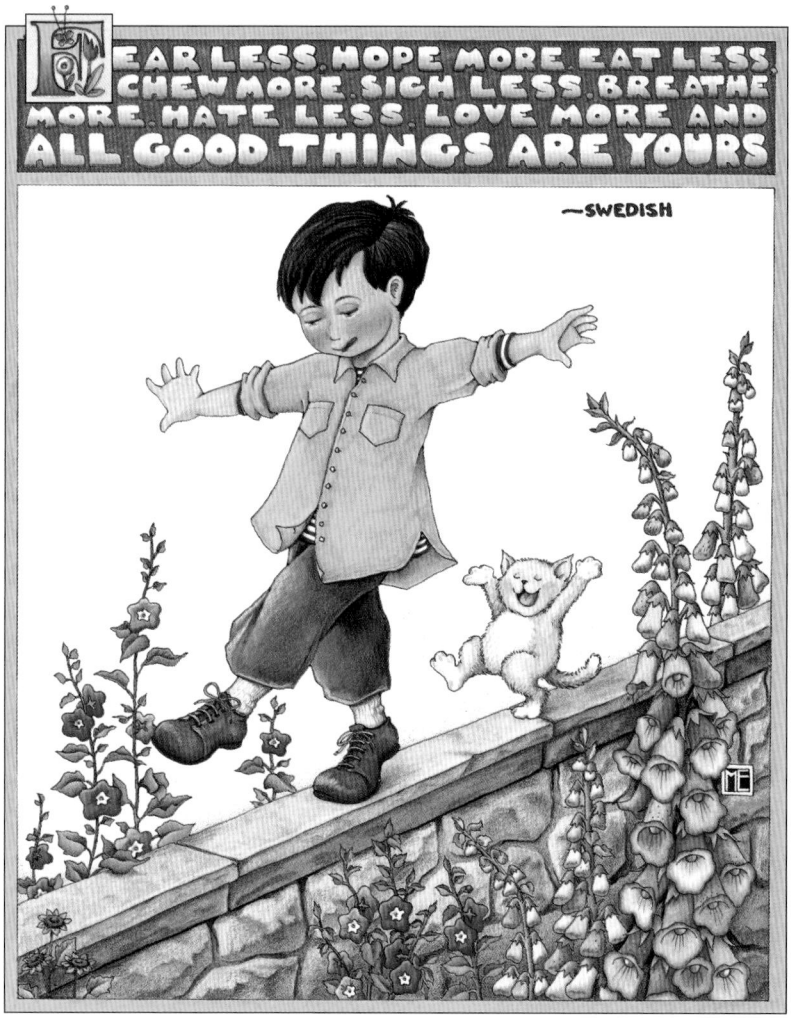
FEAR LESS, HOPE MORE, EAT LESS,
CHEW MORE, SIGH LESS, BREATHE
MORE, HATE LESS, LOVE MORE AND
ALL GOOD THINGS ARE YOURS
—SWEDISH

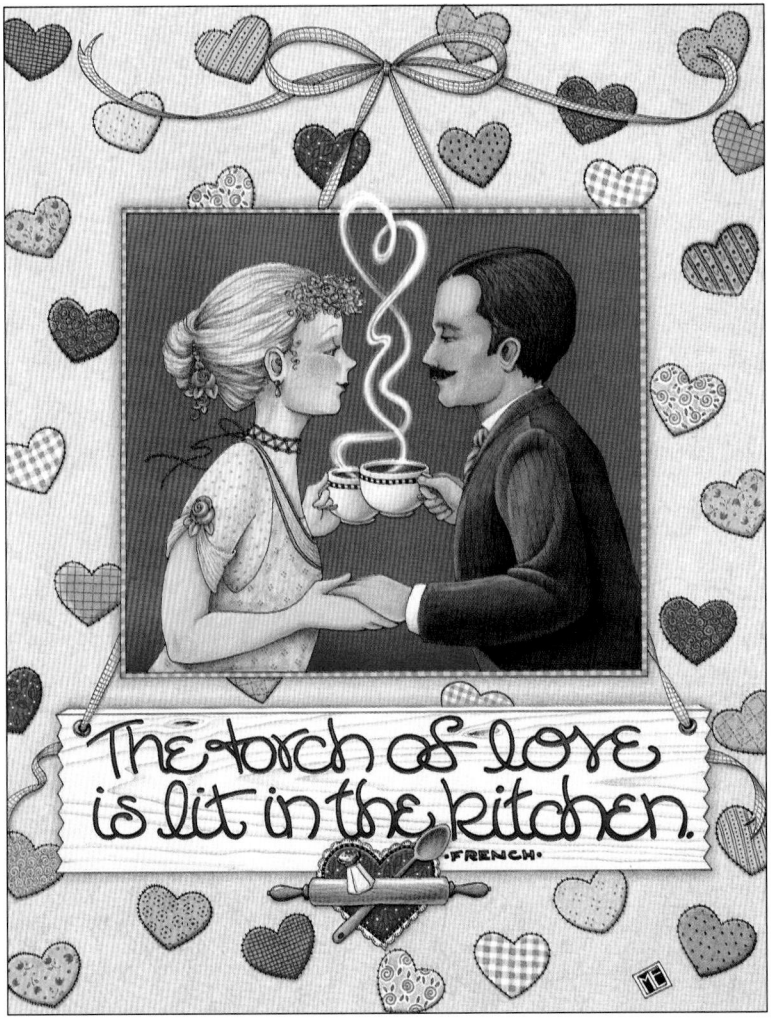
The torch of love
is lit in the kitchen.
·FRENCH·

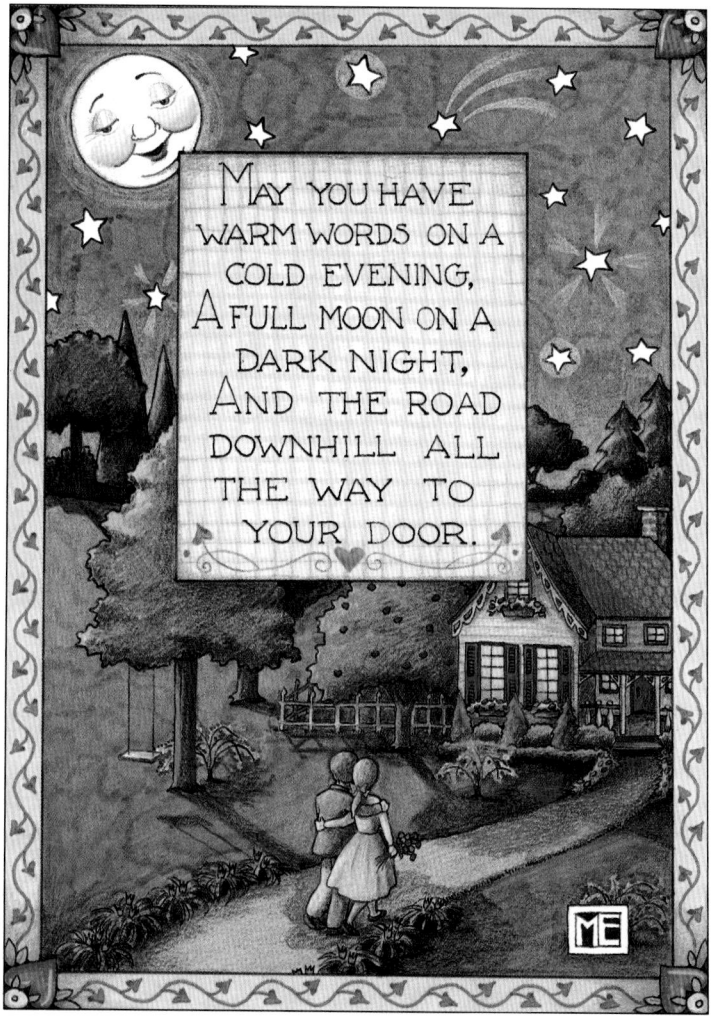
MAY YOU HAVE
WARM WORDS ON A
COLD EVENING,
A FULL MOON ON A
DARK NIGHT,
AND THE ROAD
DOWNHILL ALL
THE WAY TO
YOUR DOOR.
ME

Learning is weightless,
a treasure you can always carry easily.
–Chinese proverb

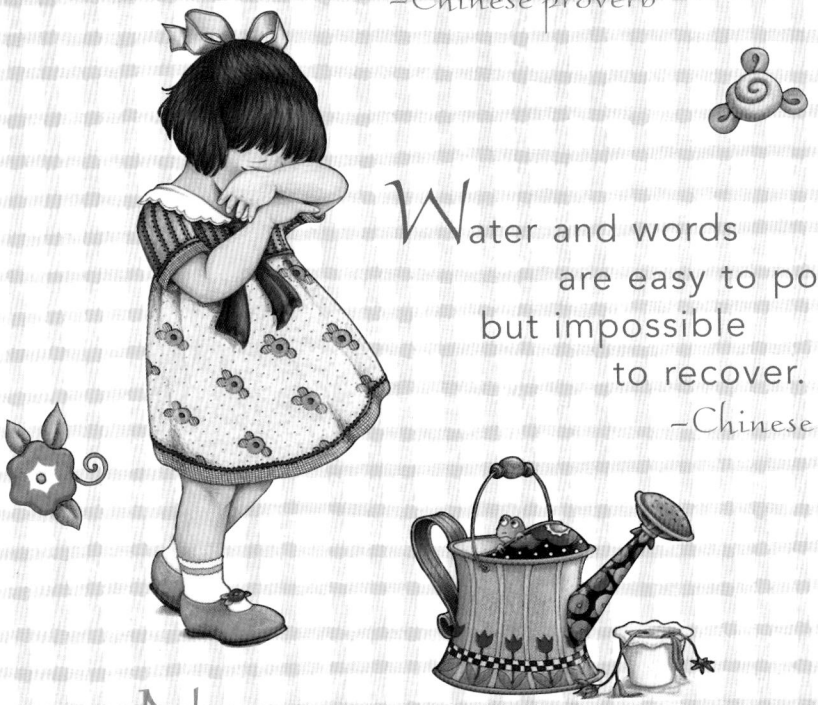

Water and words
are easy to pour
but impossible
to recover.
–Chinese proverb

Not to know is bad . . .
but not to wish to know is worse.
–West African proverb

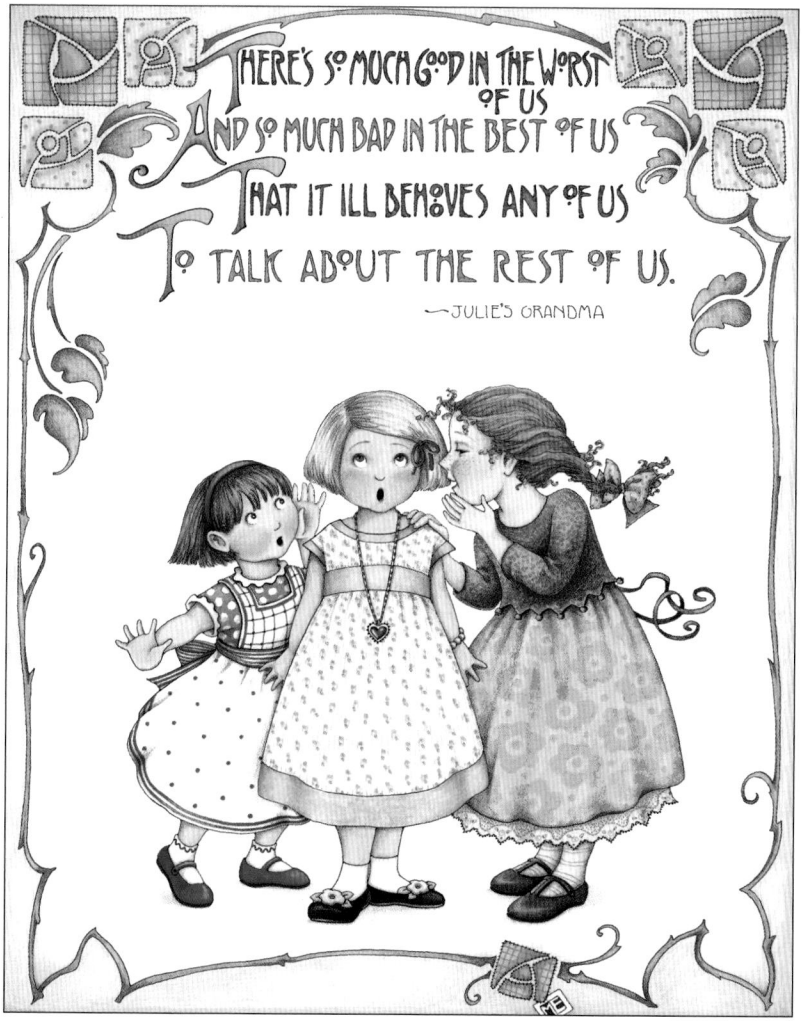
THERE'S SO MUCH GOOD IN THE WORST OF US
AND SO MUCH BAD IN THE BEST OF US
THAT IT ILL BEHOVES ANY OF US
TO TALK ABOUT THE REST OF US.
—JULIE'S GRANDMA

If you don't like something, change it.
If you can't change it,
change the way you think about it!

A journey of a thousand miles
begins with
a single step.
–Chinese proverb

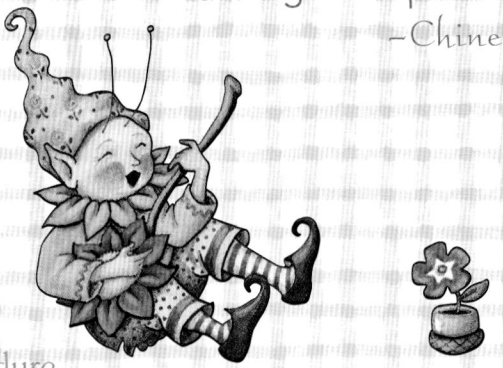

Endure,
and keep yourself for days of happiness.

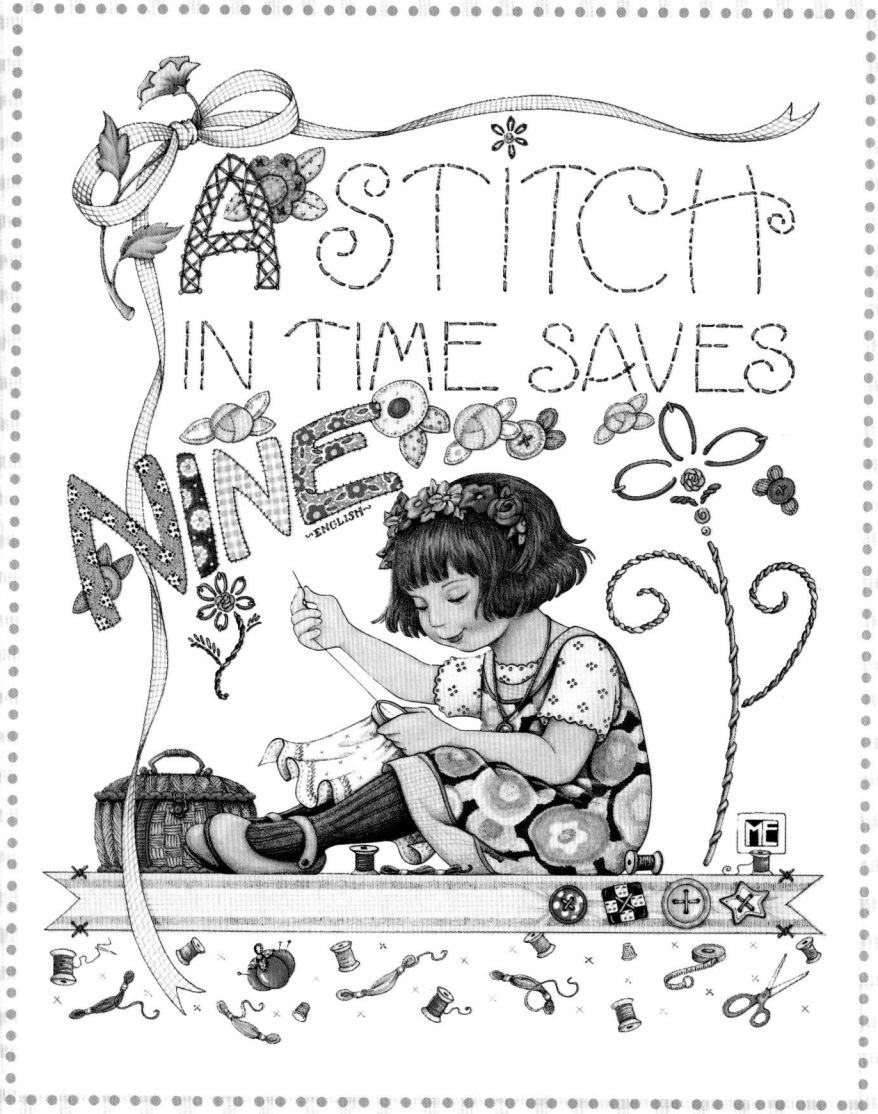
A STITCH
IN TIME SAVES
NINE
~ENGLISH~
MC

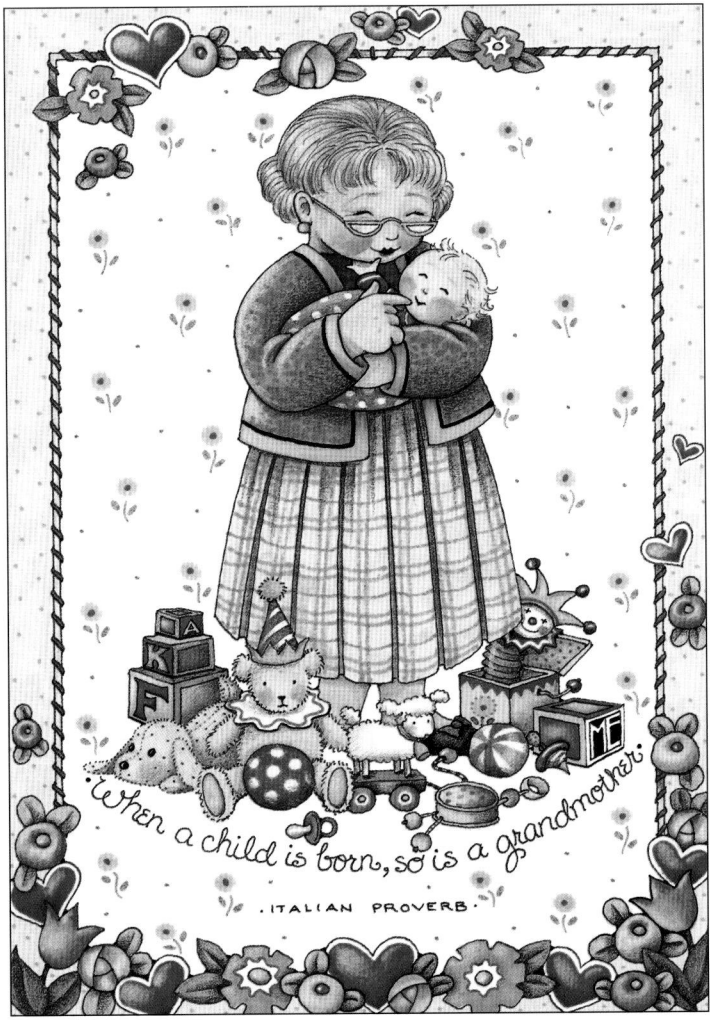
A
K
F
MC
"When a child is born, so is a grandmother."
. ITALIAN PROVERB .

Who takes the child by the hand
takes the mother by the heart.
–Danish proverb

Happiness is made to be shared.
–French proverb

The heart that loves
is always young.
–Greek proverb

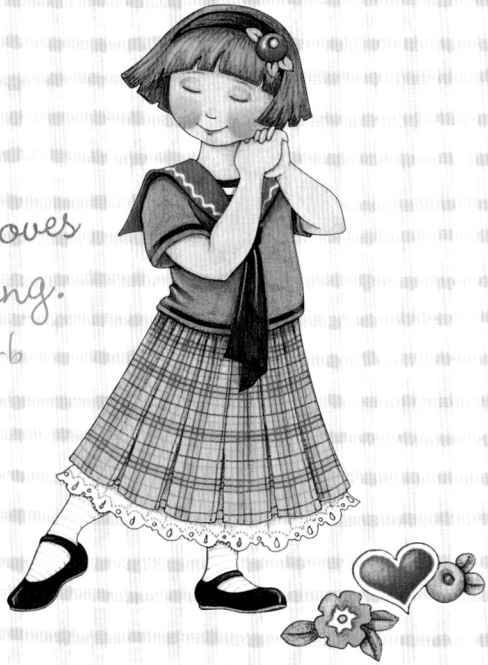

Kind hearts are the gardens;
kind thoughts are the roots;
kind words are the flowers;
kind deeds are the fruits.
—English proverb

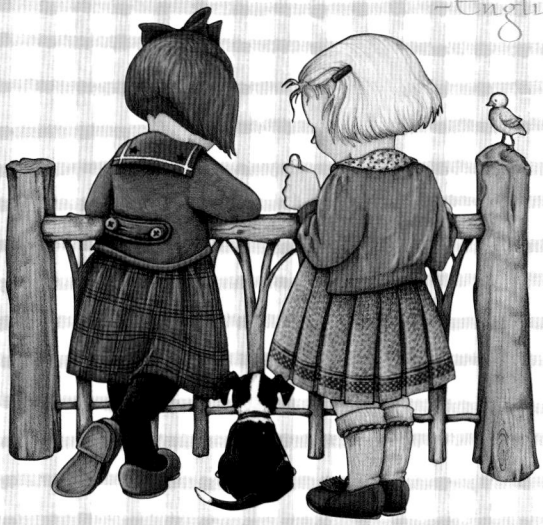

A life without a friend is a life without sun.
—French proverb

Keep company with those
who make you better.
—English saying

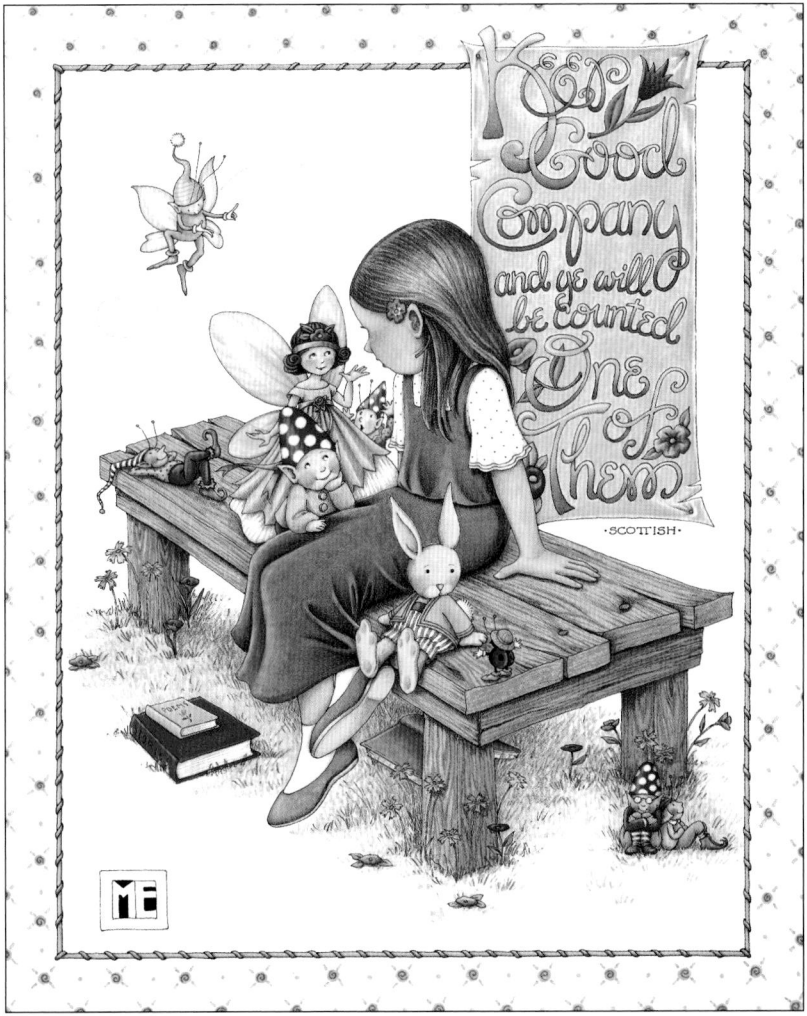
Keep Good Company and ye will be counted One of them
·SCOTTISH·

Be happy with
what you have
and you will
have *plenty*
to be
happy about.

–Irish proverb

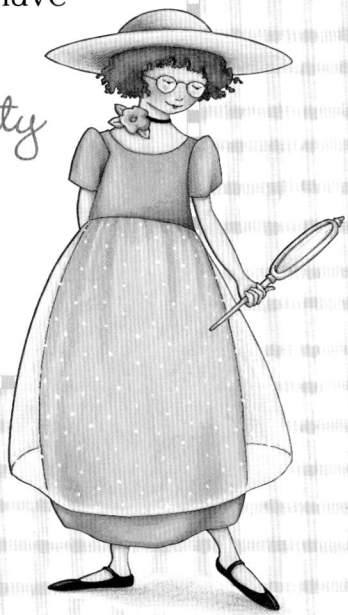

Virtue is fairer
than beauty.

–English proverb

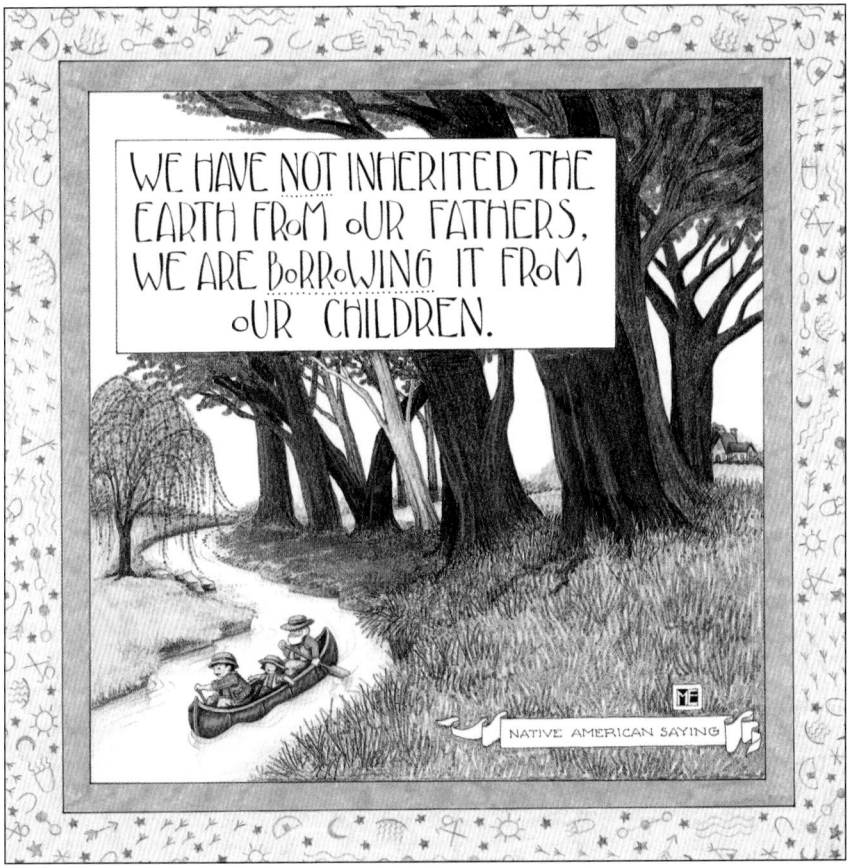
WE HAVE NOT INHERITED THE EARTH FROM OUR FATHERS. WE ARE BORROWING IT FROM OUR CHILDREN.
NATIVE AMERICAN SAYING

ife has value only when it has some
hing valuable as its object life...put your heart in
ife's too mysterious...don't take it serious! to be happy
don't do whatever you like; lik
whatever you do don't let thing ever be ordina
he greatest life is doin
what people annot do life
hat you make of it do good, be goo
or something every mother is a working woma
emember, no matter where you go.
here you are a girl's best friend is her mother th
golden opportunity you are seekin
s in yourself it's good to be queen let go, go o
our first teacher is our own heart litt

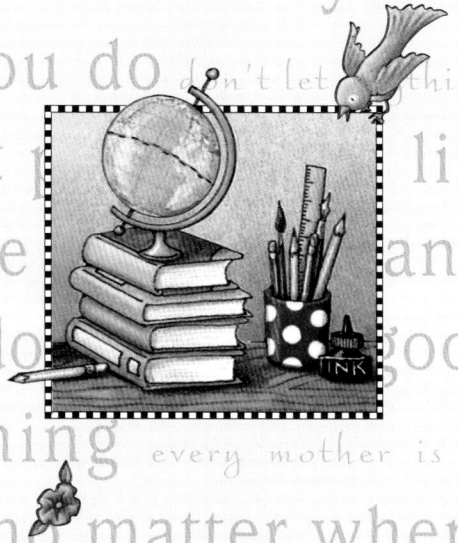

if your ship hasn'

...from folk wisdom

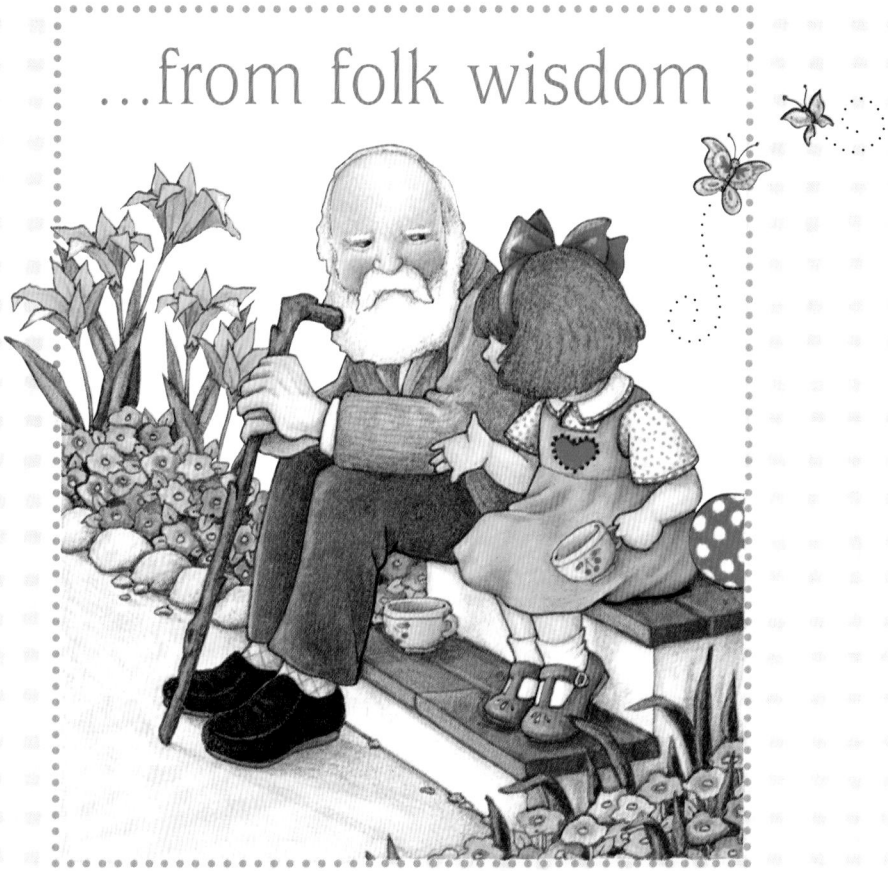

The heart is the real fountain of youth.

—Mark Twain

It's good
to be queen.

Life...
put your heart in it.

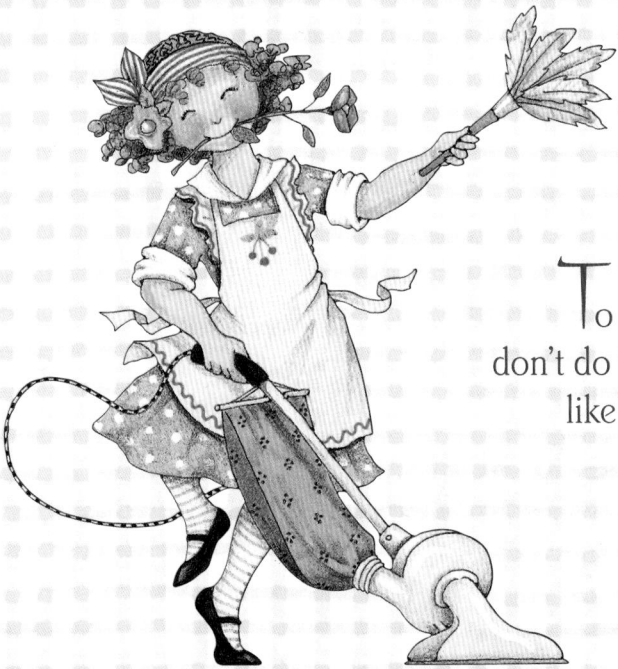

To be happy,
don't do whatever you like;
like whatever you do.

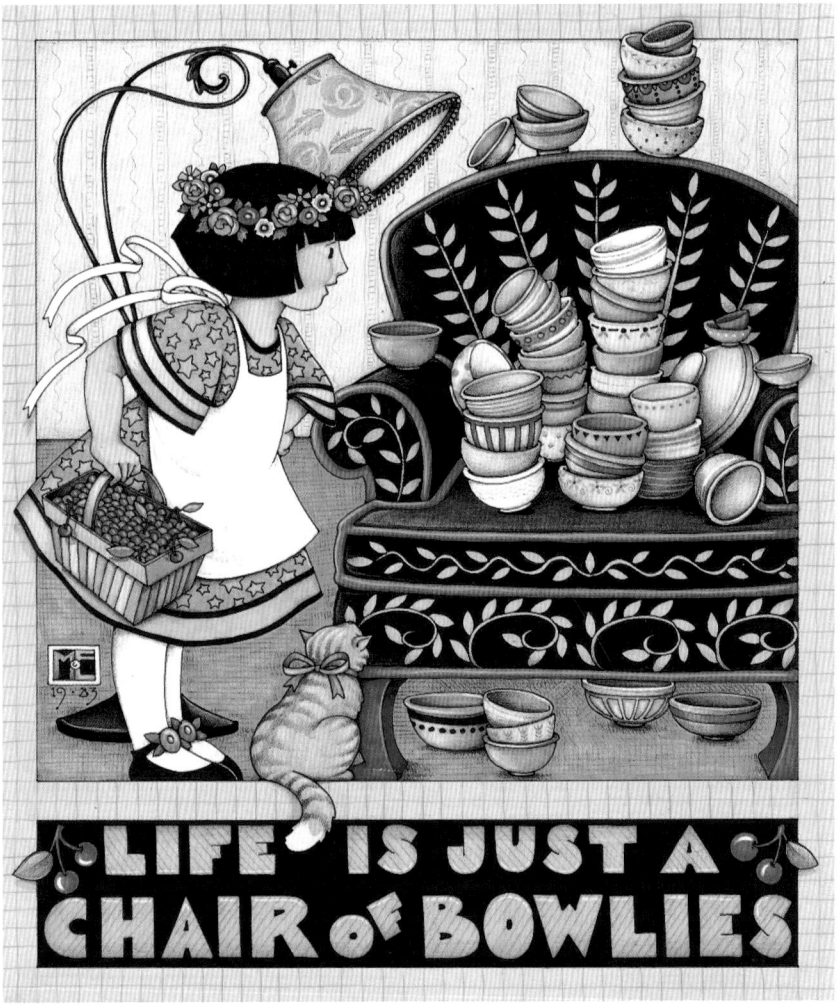
LIFE IS JUST A
CHAIR OF BOWLIES

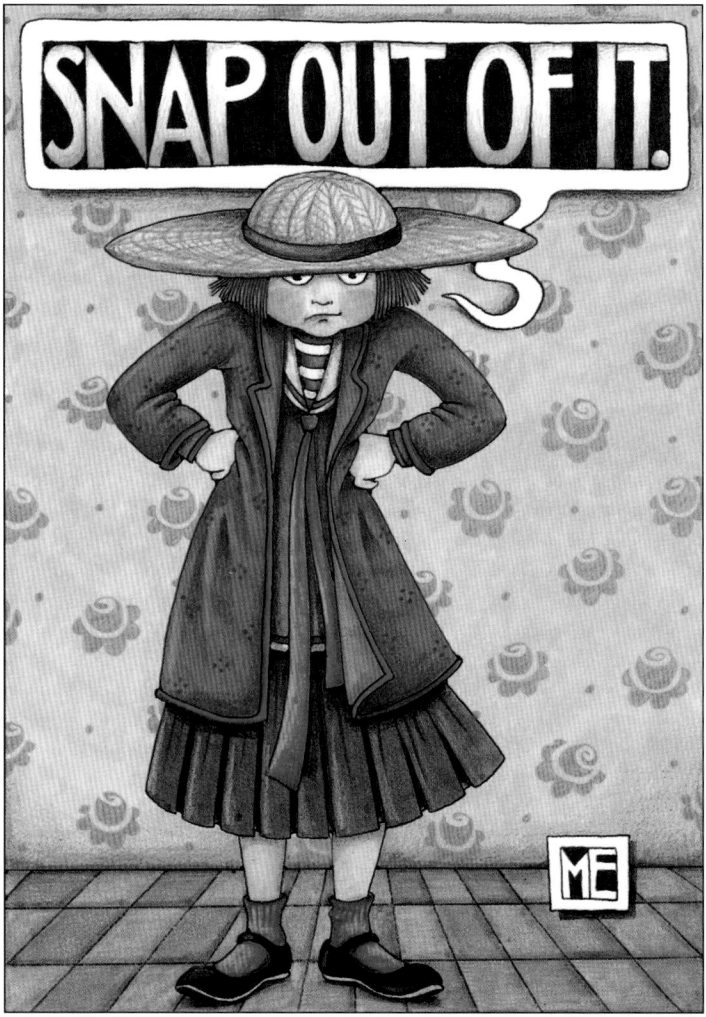
SNAP OUT OF IT.
ME

If you pray for rain,
be prepared
to deal with some mud.

The only people that never fail
are those who never try.

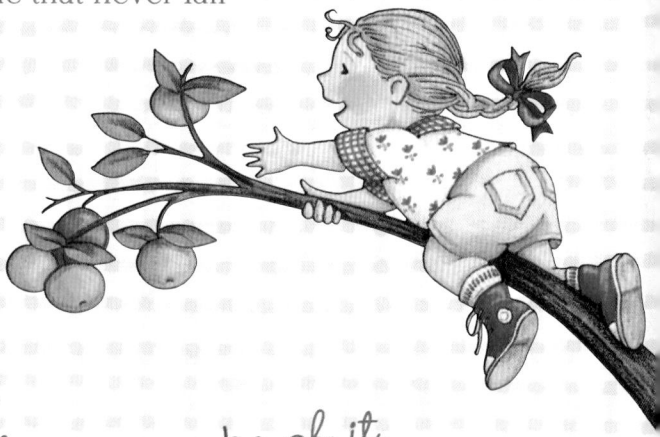

Life is what you make of it.

Remember,
no matter where you go...
there you are.

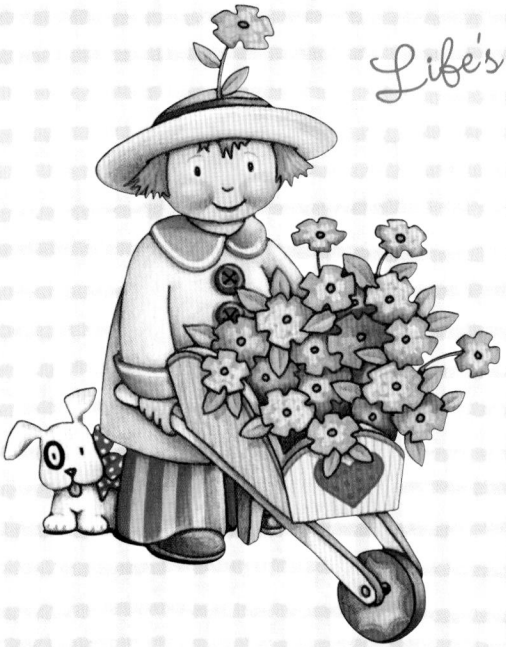

Life's too mysterious...
don't take it serious!

If your ship
hasn't come in—
swim out to it!

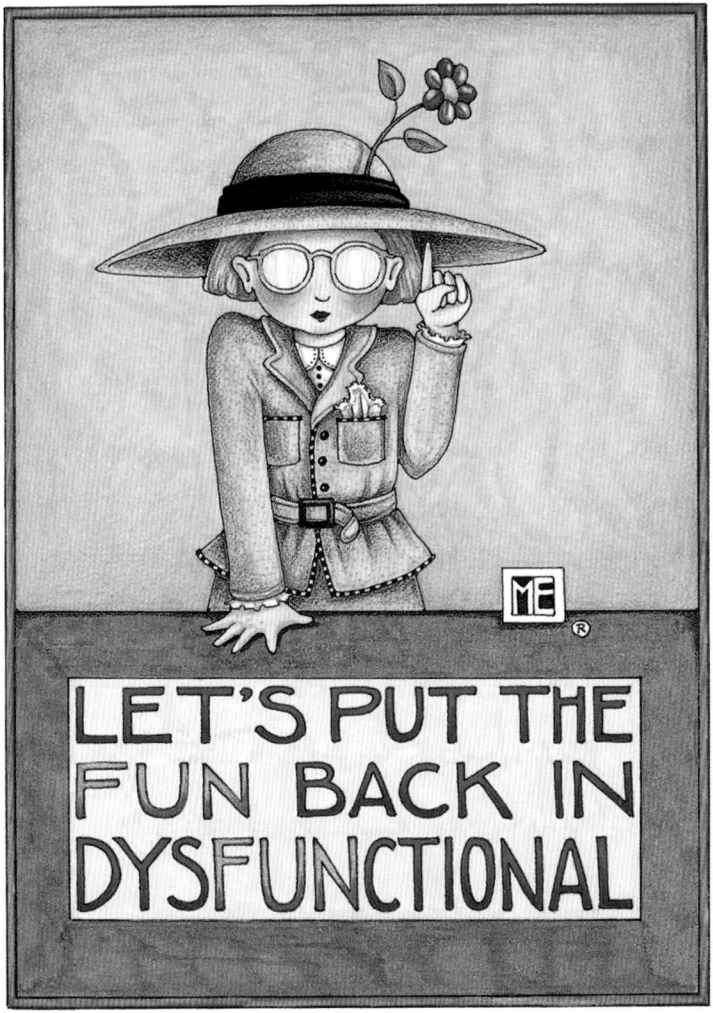
ME
LET'S PUT THE
FUN BACK IN
DYSFUNCTIONAL

The greatest pleasure in life
is doing what people say
you cannot do.

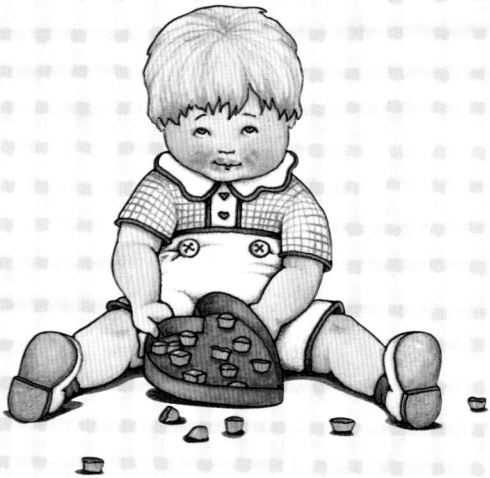

Don't let anything ever be ordinary.

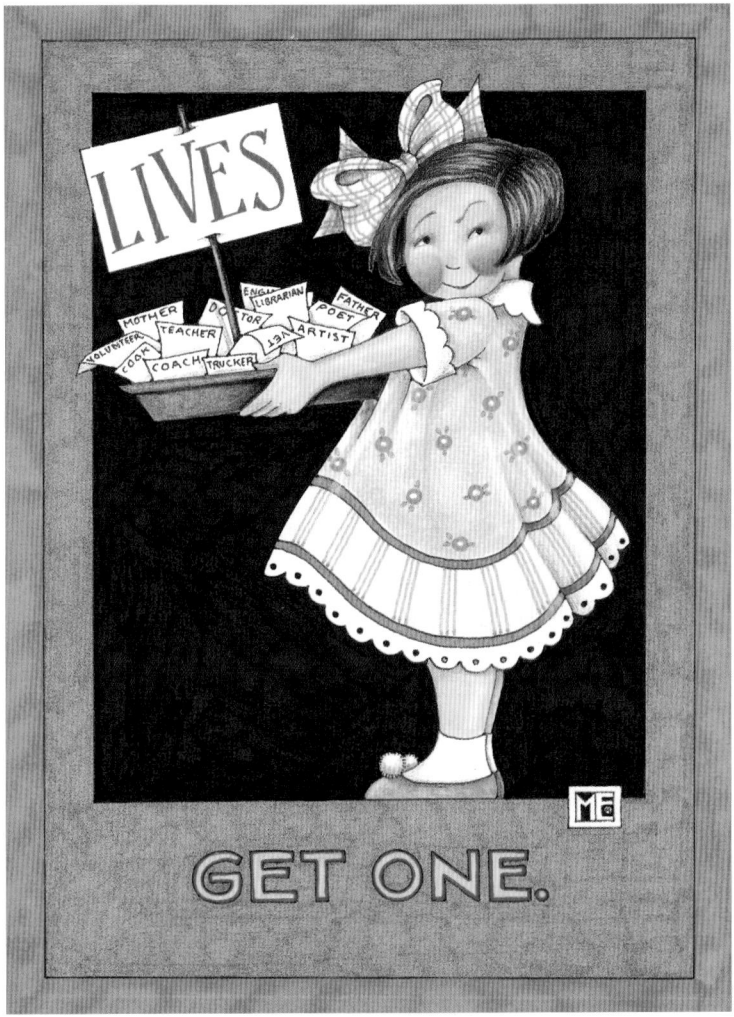
LIVES
MOTHER
VOLUNTEER
TEACHER
COOK
COACH
TRUCKER
DOCTOR
ENGINEER
LIBRARIAN
FATHER
POET
ARTIST
GET ONE.

Every mother
is a **working** woman.

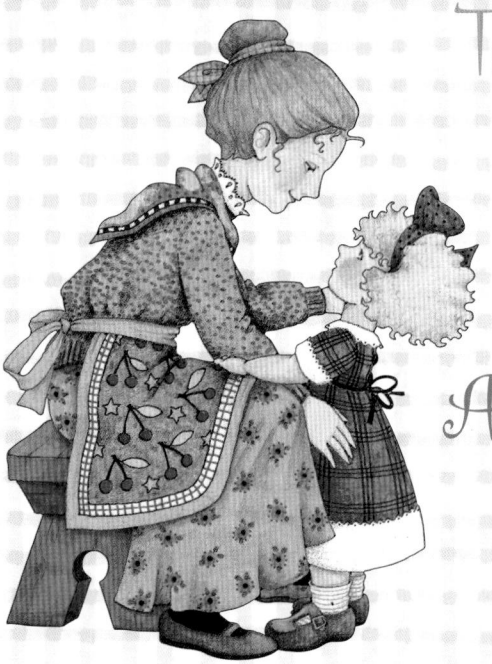

This woman
deserves a party.

A girl's best friend
is her mother.

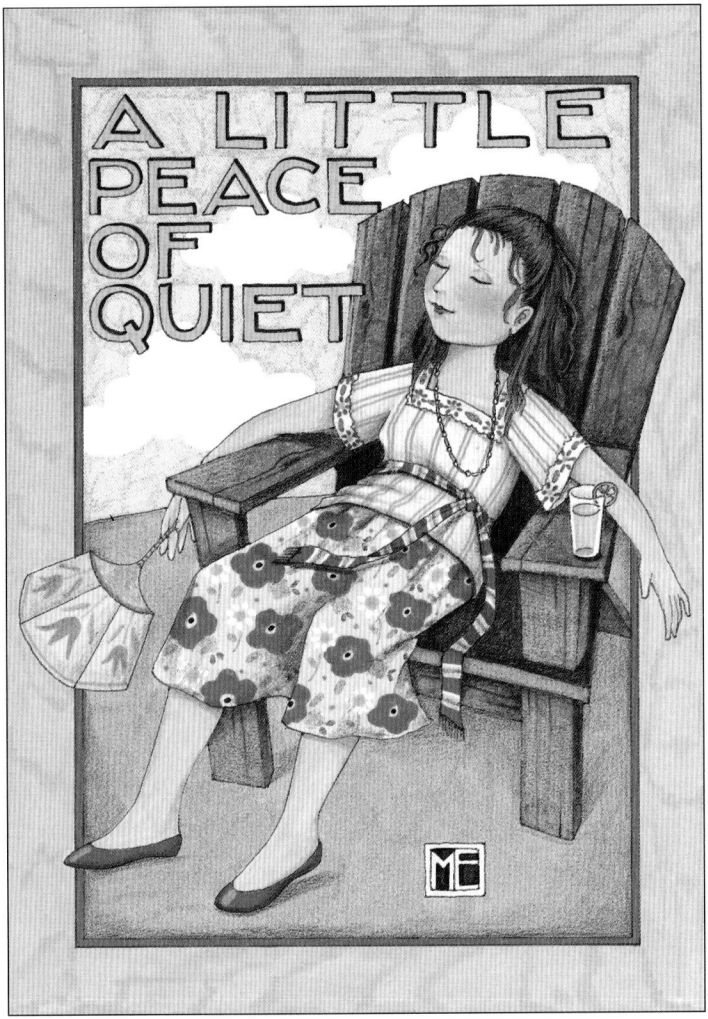
A LITTLE
PEACE
OF
QUIET
MC

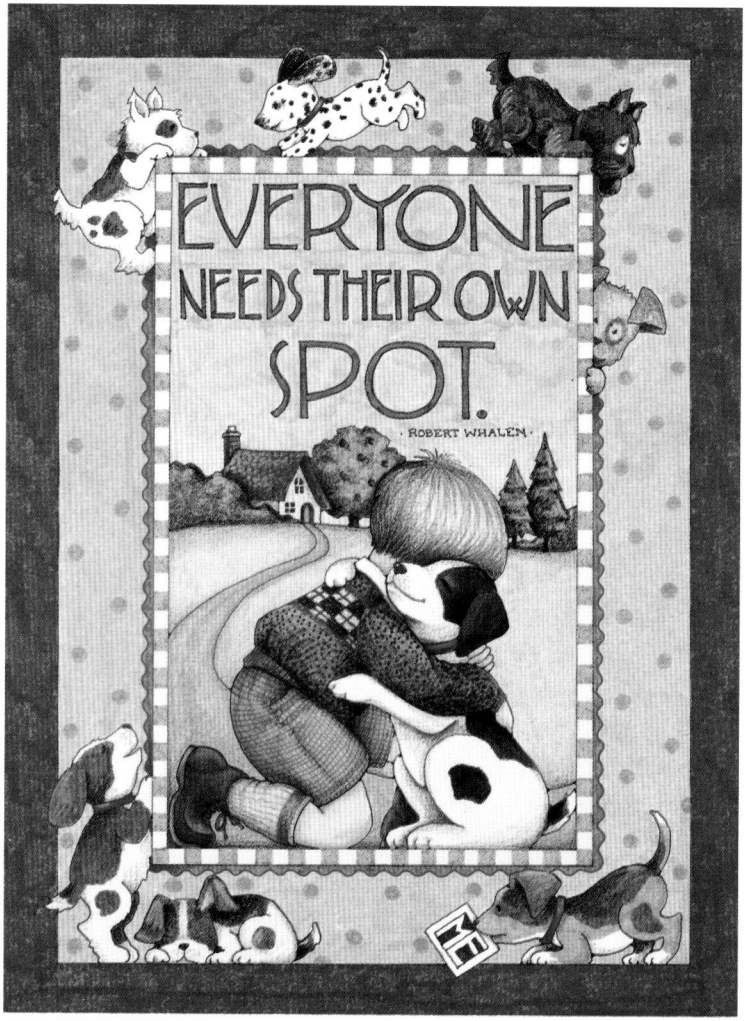
EVERYONE
NEEDS THEIR OWN
SPOT.
ROBERT WHALEN

The golden opportunity
you are seeking
is in yourself.

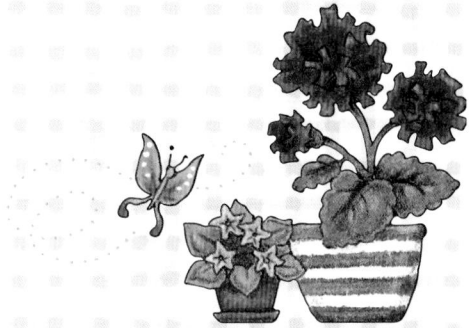

Bloom where you're planted.

Worrying does not
empty tomorrow of its troubles,
it empties today of its strength.

mary engelbreit

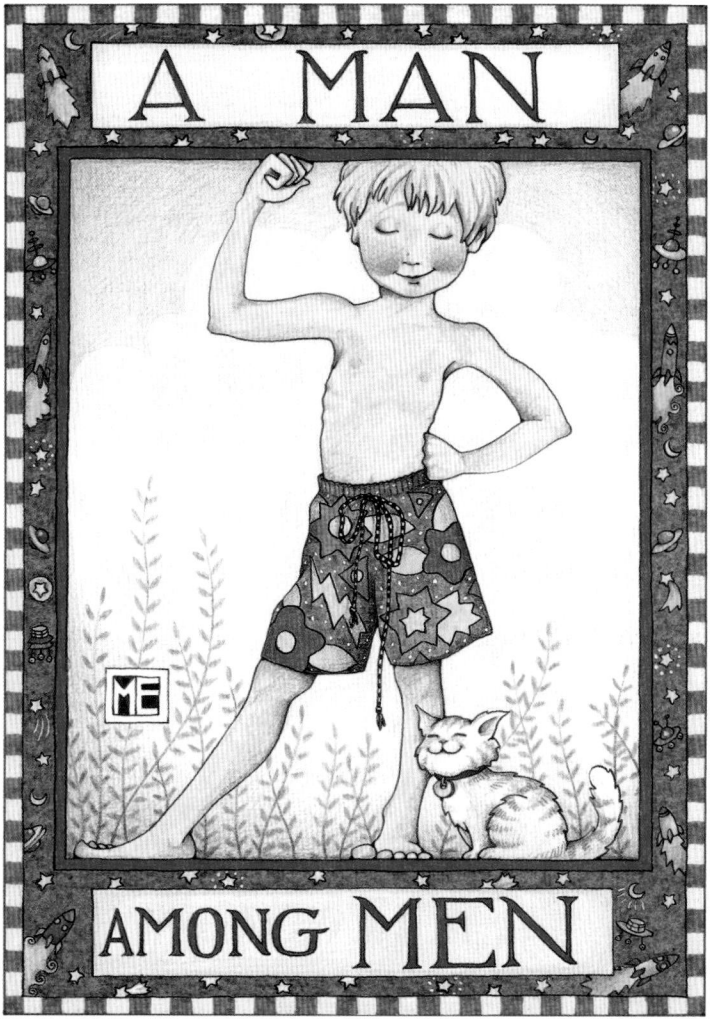

Life has value
only when it has something
valuable as its object.

Don't just be good,
be good
for something.

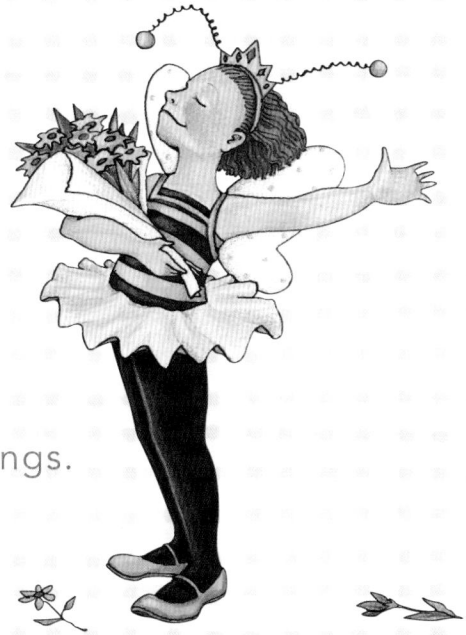

Little minds
achieve
great things.

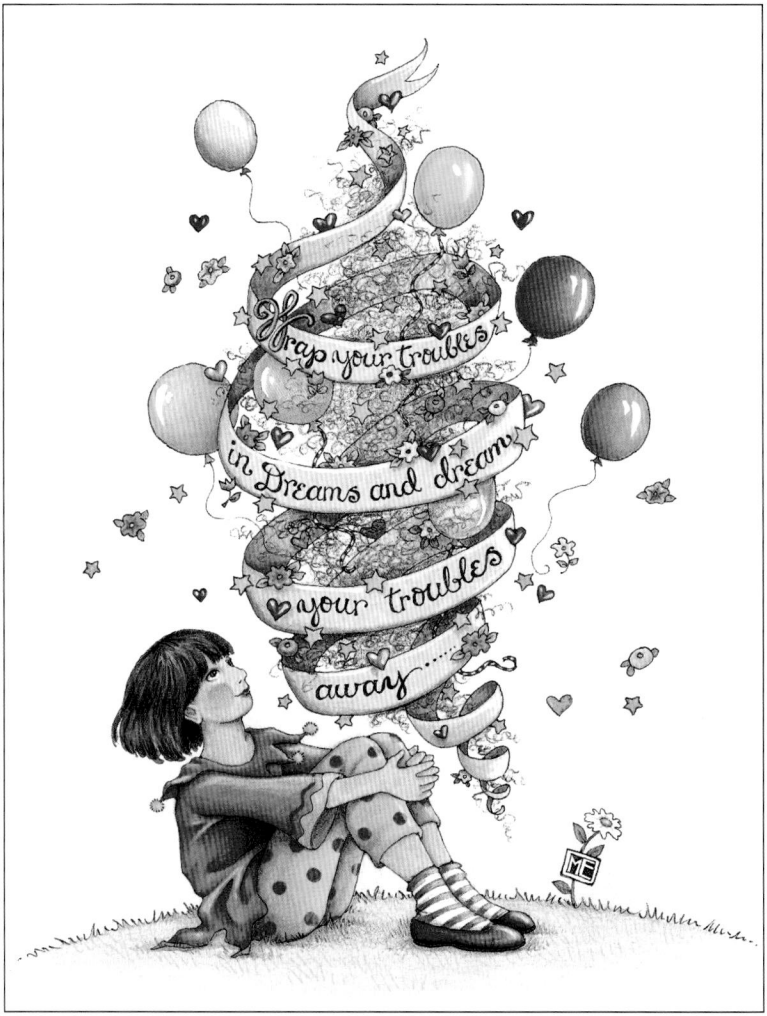
If you trap your troubles
in Dreams and dream
your troubles
away.....
ME

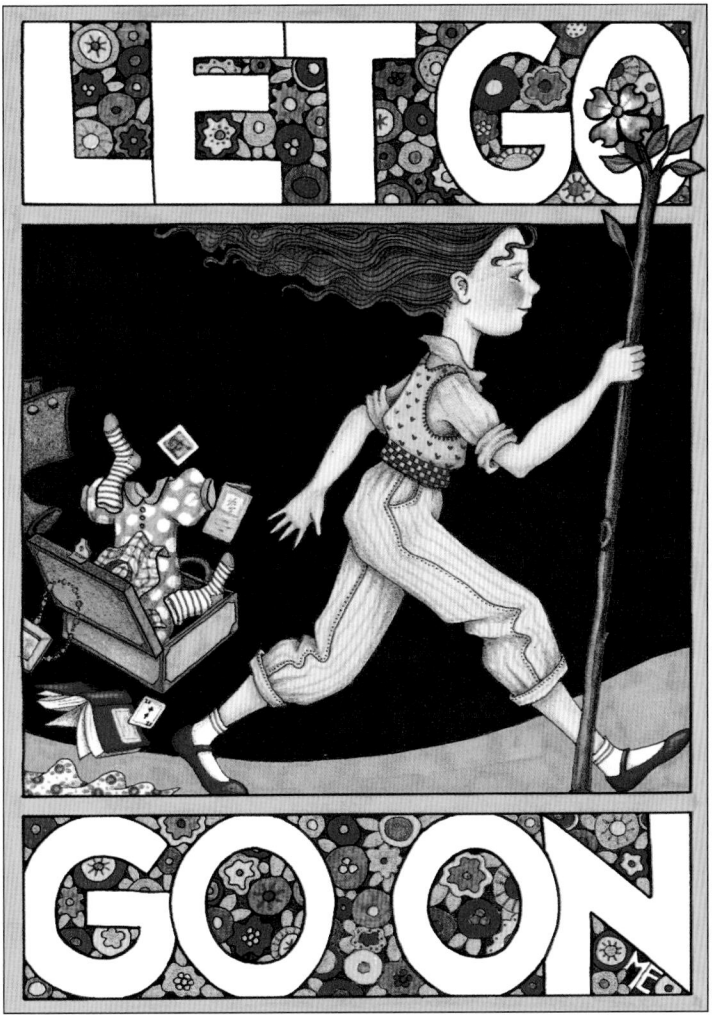
LET GO
GO ON
ME

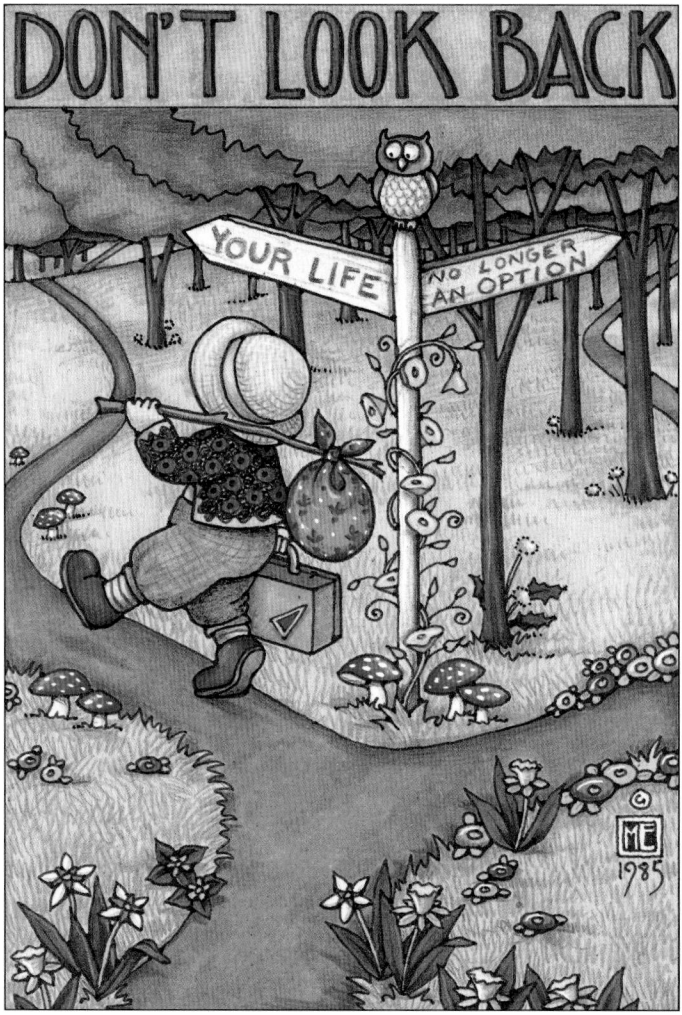
DON'T LOOK BACK
YOUR LIFE
NO LONGER AN OPTION
ME
1985